Y0-DKP-677

Intimacy

Intimacy:
The Essence of Male and Female

by
Shirley Gehrke Luthman

Nash Publishing
Los Angeles

Library of Congress Catalog Card Number: 72-81832
Standard Book Number: 8402-1282-8

Published simultaneously in the United States and Canada
by Nash Publishing Corporation, 9255 Sunset Boulevard,
Los Angeles, California 90069.

Printed in the United States of America.

First Printing.

In Memory

*To my husband, Merrill Joseph Luthman,
and my father, Samuel Ernest Gehrke—
who taught me most of the good things
I know about men.*

Contents

Part One:

The Essence
of Male and Female

Chapter One:

Whys and Wherefores

As a therapist, my special interest has been to explore and understand the reasons for the breakdowns in marital and family relationships. That exploration has led me into exciting discoveries about the essence of maleness and femaleness, the potential for enhancement and aliveness within the male-female connections, and the possibilities for unleashing tremendous creative power within ourselves as we let go of our distortions about our identity (what is a relationship and how to achieve it). Tremendous energy is locked into our struggles to conform to some idealized, unrealistic image of who we should be and how we should behave in order to survive, be successful, and be loved.

I do not believe that we can accurately classify people emotionally within categories like "sick" or "well." If, instead, we look at people in terms of their growth, there are people who are growing and producing and creating in ways that are fitting for them. Such a person seems to be connected to an inner rhythm or flow that is uniquely his own. He marches to his own drummer. Unfortunately, we have operated in our culture as though such dedication to one's own uniqueness requires the sacrifice of a deep love connection and, perhaps, the price of ostracism by the group. Our fear of our own uniqueness has led us to avoid expressing our innermost feelings, or to express them in ways that are inadequate or distorted. Such ways are developed to mask or hide what we really feel; or, to pretend we feel something else so we will be more acceptable to others and therefore not be hurt. As a result of this process of masking or hiding feelings, individual growth is blocked in one or more areas and symptoms evolve. I see most physical, mental, marital, and family breakdowns as indications that growth is being blocked in the individual, marital connection, or family unit. The human organism has to grow or die. Growth is always blocked in some way when feelings are blocked. Maximum growth for the individual is dependent on his capacity to express who he is—which means his feelings—clearly, congruently, and spontaneously.

I do not believe that therapists change people. We observe and then make explicit the nature of the negative processes (ways of functioning) which defeat them. These are the processes which defeat the individual's growth by covering and denying who he is rather than expressing himself in a spontaneous, congruent, and thus, enhancing way. As therapists, we explore with people how and for what reasons these negative processes were learned; and we weigh with them the pros and cons of letting go of these old processes to begin a search for new ways which fit them better.

There are risks in committing oneself to grow. Inherent in growth is the greatest excitement in life, but growth produces constant change, and change is often frightening because it always leads us into the unknown. When the individual, aware of the risks, has made his choice, then we teach him new processes for developing a better understanding of himself, for expressing himself more congruently and spontaneously, for making connections that are enhancing to himself and others, and for adapting to constant change.

I am intensely involved in the exploration of these positive growth processes both for myself and the people with whom I work, because I feel my commitment to growth must be equal to theirs. I do not see myself as some God-Expert handing down maxims about life from my exalted position of "having arrived." I see myself, in the flow of my own growth, contributing to the growth of others by letting them experience who I am as a person. At the same time, others are contributing to my growth by allowing me to experience who they really are. This is true of all my connections—client, friend, family—whatever the relationship. The nature of the relationship may be different, but the process is the same. The process is the mutual enhancement of each other's growth by the open expression of each other's thoughts, feelings, sensations, perceptions, cognitions, assumptions, conclusions, limitations, and demands as it fits the framework of the relationship.

Such exploration has led me to the first stage of discovery which I will describe to you in the next pages. I do not propose this book to be fact or the result of pure scientific research. It is an expression of the theories I have evolved based on my own experience, personal and professional. Professionally, over the past fifteen years, I have observed and explored hundreds of marital relationships and the many facets of male and female identity. To save time and space, I use the term "marital" or "husband-wife" or "marriage" to include all intimate male-female relationships, legal or otherwise. Personally, I have made a few forays into the infinite variety of connections a woman can make with men and, because of the nature of who I am, my observer-self has always accompanied my participant-self. My interest has been to explore, in ever-expanding depth, the mystery of maleness and femaleness and the possible means of self-expression by which each might enhance the other. I have arrived at some perceptions that I would like to share, not as conclusions or a finished product, but simply as comment about the current stage in my unfolding exploratory process into the always fascinating, sometimes awesome, nature of who we are.

Chapter Two:

What Males
and Females Are Not

In our culture, maleness and femaleness have been defined around externals: roles, sensory data (dress, mannerisms, speech, habits), performance, sexual capacity, emotional expression, and sexual preference.

A. Roles. Historically, men have hunted, chopped wood, fought wars, been mechanics, explorers, moneymakers, and risk takers. Any man who would do any one of these things well could comfortably attach his masculinity to the function. In this way, he gained comfort since he had obviously proved his maleness to everyone through what he could produce. However, he paid a tremendous price in that his focus on production as the essence of his maleness cut him off from exploring all the other parts of himself, either because he didn't have time or energy or because they might not fit the image he had affected. He sacrificed the richness of his total person on the altar of gain. I do not mean to imply that all these forms of production cannot be creative and an expression of growth and joy. They can, but not when they are perceived by the individual as the validation of his identity as a male. In that context production becomes a trap.

Women, traditionally, have tended and feathered the nest. They have gained a safe haven, but lost their creativity. They have associated exploration and risk-taking with masculinity and aloneness, and passivity with femininity—the velvet trap.

Interactionally, the male production trap and the female velvet trap produce, at worst, resentment and frustration in the male-female relationship for which each blames the other. Even at best, the traps encourage the sexes not to trust each other. For example, as the wife, I'm afraid to leave my trap because if I begin to assert myself and be different than I have been you may leave me. As the husband, I'm afraid that if I begin to open up all my feelings to you, wife, you may not think I'm masculine and therefore not respect me. So, free and flowing exploration between males and females is hampered or prevented entirely.

B. Sensory Data. We have established criteria to determine maleness and femaleness at a glance or momentary encounter by such evidence as:

1. Dress: Length and style of hair, height of heels and style of shoe, plainness or elaborateness of costume, use of makeup (including perfumes, skin softeners and deodorants), and use of materials and color.

2. Mannerisms: Walk, gestures, posture of body.

3. Speech: Use of "cuss" words, tone, range of sound.

4. Habits: Smoking, chewing tobacco, whistling.

We are becoming less rigid in these areas, but are far from exploding the myth that such superficial criteria have anything at all to do with sexual identity. By our emphasis on such meaningless externals, we have communicated to our children and each other a powerful implied message that the superficial aspects of a relationship carry vast importance. Such emphasis on the superficial protects us from having to put ourselves on the line about who we really are and explore ourselves in depth in relation to each other. It also produces boredom, disillusionment, and the death of relationships.

C. Performance. Physical daring and endurance have long been connected with masculinity. I believe that precious myth has resulted in men and women both contributing blithely to the destruction of the male of the species. The myth pervades seemingly simple functions like who does most of the auto driving when men and women are together. The choice is not based on who has the most energy at the time or on sharing the chore. He's the male; ergo, he drives. It is equally true that we assign certain tasks to the female, such as grocery shopping or baby-sitting. However, it seems to me that so many of the male-oriented tasks are more stressful and tension producing.

In reality, the male has more powerful musculature than the female and a frame that gives him better leverage for lifting, throwing, and hitting. Those assets make it possible for him to lift heavier objects, throw farther, and hit harder. Endurance is related to being in top physical condition and is individually determined, not sex related. In addition, emotional strength is an individual matter and, as far as I can determine, not at all sex-related. Physical daring has long been a dangerous and destructive way for males in our society to prove their masculinity. If it ceased to be a criterion for maleness, then we could determine whether or not it is really sex-related in any way. There are individuals, male and female, who risk themselves physically, not to prove something or out of an unconscious death wish, but because physical risk makes them feel most alive. In the film *Le Mans*, someone asked Steve McQueen, playing a racing driver, what made him risk his life just to drive a car faster than anyone else. He replied, in effect, that he was totally alive when he was racing that car and the rest of life was "just waiting." The sense of total aliveness is something like a drug—so exhilarating that the risks may lose importance by comparison.

D. Sexual Capacity. The myths about males and females in the area of sexual capacity are so distorted and powerful, I don't know if we will ever discover the full truth. Both males and females often equate masculinity with the size of a man's penis and with his sexual prowess—i.e., ability to have frequent erections, maintain an erection at length, and bring the female to orgasm. The fallacy in this kind of equation is that it splits the outside functioning from each individual's internal process. As an example, the male's dialogue within himself during intercourse might go something like this:

> *Look at the expression on her face—she really thinks I'm great. Well, I'll show her—here's another orgasm coming up, baby!*

Or:

> *Oh God, I can feel myself failing—I hope she's satisfied or I'll never hear the end of it, the bitch.*

The sexual act becomes a performance rather than the self-expression and feeling flow between two people. Many people in our culture do operate basically as though they were split in this way. An individual adopts an outer façade based on what is right, good, will please others, or will prevent rocking the boat in the relationship. What he is really feeling on the inside may be totally different most of the time from what he is showing outwardly. In fact, he may be

10

so used to this facade that he may not even know what he is really feeling. Many of the "studs" fall into this category They are so successfully split that they can perform like machines and their feelings never get in the way. The price they pay for that split is the inability to feel deeply or to develop deep relationships.

If the male is concerned with his feeling expression rather than performance, his focus will be on the flow of feeling between himself and his partner. He will allow himself to lose himself in his experience of warmth, pleasure, or whatever emerges. Sometimes the experience of physical intimacy may begin with lust and lead to the opening up of other feelings like sadness or pain or other feelings related to other situations or people. If the individuals involved are focused on feeling, they can go with whatever emerges and experience a flow with each other that is rewarding no matter where it leads. If they are committed to performance, they have a program about how sex should go and the natural flow is cut off. This makes sex a chore, not an experience.

I am convinced that we have no realistic knowledge about what males are capable of sexually because most males in our culture express their sexuality according to a program of performance. I think that if they learned to experience sex as part of their self-expression and as a result of a flow between the male and female, our whole concept of male sexuality would change. For example, I believe that any male who expresses his sexuality out of who he is and out of his own natural flow would be capable of sexual expression until the day he dies, barring physical injury or incapacitating illness. The male who is tied to performance begins to lose ground sexually as his youth fades because performance, as in any sport, is based on physical youth and fitness. I think the male whose sexuality is a constant expression of his insides gets better and better with age in terms of greater satisfaction to himself and his partner.

The individual whose body, mind, and feelings are all connected to each other so that he goes into any experience as a whole person, does not have total control over his body's performance. He cannot say "Perform!" and have it obey. His body performance is determined by his health, alertness, internal feeling state, and the feelings he is perceiving from his partner. So, if he wants to make love and his body doesn't cooperate—no erection, no sustained erection, premature ejaculation—he doesn't ask "What's wrong with me?" Instead, he accepts that his body is talking to him, saying something to which he needs to attend. Perhaps it's saying, he's been pushing himself harder than he thought and he needs to take better care of himself; or, maybe it's saying something about the relationship. Maybe there are unresolved feelings between him and his partner that are getting in the way. If he checks his insides and can't find any leftover, unspoken feelings, he may be perceiving something from his wife. People communicate by "vibrations" as well as by words and body messages. A small infant perceives his mother's tension when she's holding him and starts to cry, leaving the parents bewildered because they can't find any obvious reason for his discomfort. We do not lose this ability to perceive someone else's insides when we are physically close to him or her. Most people don't trust, appreciate, or understand that ability and tend to ignore messages that come via that channel. Because of this distrust of the intangible, we don't even have a word for this kind of supraperception. However, our bodies still perceive and respond on that level even if our heads ignore such phenomena. With the couple I've been describing, the wife may be sending out two messages. Her words and body may be saying "I want to make love"; her insides may be feeling some resentment toward her husband which she hasn't expressed. He is perceiving contradictory messages on two different levels, in effect, "Go away, come close," and his body is responding by withdrawing or withholding.

Historically, the female has been so repressed sexually that it is a miracle she is still interested. She still is tremendously repressed sexually by culture. The truly sexually assertive female is yet a freak in our society, seldom appreciated and even distrusted by both men and women. Few women are at all honest about their sexuality. Interactionally, such emphasis on performance by males and lack of performance by females has made people so afraid to be who they are that many human beings have missed out on one of the most exciting explorations life has to offer. I wonder, for example, in how many male-female relationships the male has been able to be totally passive, for a change, and the female able to be totally the aggressor and make love to him. That can be a very enlightening and rewarding experience for both, yet it is taboo culturally. Because of our distortions about sex, I don't think we have any way of knowing, at this point, whether aggressiveness or passivity in sexual behavior is sex related.

E. Emotional Expression. Crying, screaming, temper tantrums, and hysteria are rigidly attached to femaleness, while the prototype of the strong, silent, logical, reasonable male reigns supreme. I suspect that that rule of behavior, plus external stress, are strong factors in what I consider to be an epidemic of heart disease among reasonably young males in our present society. Implicit in that whole framework is the suggestion that strong, intelligent, dependable people do not cry, scream, have temper tantrums, or get hysterical; and people who express themselves in those ways are unreliable, not to be taken seriously, and weak. Nothing could be further from the truth. There is no rule about how any individual, male or female, should express himself or herself. What is important is that each individual find a way to express who he is inside in a way that fits his own unique personality. I know of no particular way of expressing feelings that is distinctly male or female. There are just ways that are distinctly individual.

F. Sexual Preferences. We have been so brainwashed for thousands of years into believing that real males have only female sexual partners and real females have only male sexual partners that I don't think we have any idea what the reality is. I suspect that we are actually bisexual in terms of physical exploration. Without our taboos, I think there would be much fondling, touching, kissing, and holding between males and between females. The human organism is primarily contact oriented—we like and need to touch each other. Insofar as relationships are concerned, I think the male-female combination holds the greatest potential for balance between difference and sameness; and, thus, probably also the greatest potential for excitement. Because of that, I think it would survive as the primary choice for long-term relationships even if all taboos vanished. Either way, I do not think that the choice of a sexual partner—black, white, red, green, male or female—determines maleness or femaleness.

G. Male Aggressiveness and Female Passivity. This is one of the most destructive myths perpetrated on men and women. The almost wholesale cultural acceptance of the propaganda that men are primarily aggressive and women are primarily passive has forced females to use devious, manipulative ways of expressing their assertions so that the assertions don't look like what they are. This is an extremely depreciating process to the female, and thus produces escalating resentment of which she is often not aware because she has been so thoroughly brainwashed about her role. However, she takes it out on her children without even knowing it, especially on the males, who usually get the brunt of Mom's resentment about her repressed assertions. If the female is aware of this discrepancy between her cultural role and her real feelings, she often feels herself trapped. It seems to her as though she has the choice to be assertive, independent, and subsequently isolated with no one to lean on or to take care of her; or, she can be taken care of and protected at the loss of her assertive power. It is an impossible choice and society has been paying for that trap for generations.

There is a play called *The Latent Heterosexual* in which the author Paddy Chayefsky makes the point, in effect, that it is easier in our culture to be a homosexual male than to be a non-aggressive heterosexual male. The assumption that aggressiveness is evidence of maleness and passivity is an indication of femaleness makes it difficult for each to honor those parts of self that do not fit the image. The reality is that the female's appreciation of herself as a feminine person is directly connected to her ability to honor her strength as well as her tenderness. They are two sides of the same coin in her emotional makeup. If she fails to express her strength, her assertions, and her aggressiveness as it fits her to do, she reduces her ability to feel and give love because she builds resentment which gets in the way of the tender feelings.

The male can be totally confused if he is led to believe that assertion, in order to be male, must be driving, aggressive, and forceful. In order for him to feel comfortable about his maleness, he must be able to assert the parts of himself that are quiet, passive or withdrawn as well as the parts that are active. In addition, the active parts do not need to be asserted forcefully by him in order to be male. They simply must be asserted in a way that fits who he is. Aggressiveness and passivity have nothing to do with sexual identity. They have more to do with the natural rhythm of the individual, which I'll describe in detail in the next chapter.

We have clung to such rigid external categorizations as all those I've just described because they are clear, concrete, and tangible. However, men and women both are becoming increasingly aware of the price they are paying for such rigidity in the repression of individuality, creativity, and life itself.

In my work with couples and individuals, the goal is to enable the individual to define and act on his own unique insides by getting in touch with his feelings and learning how to express them in ways that are fitting to him. As the individual grows in this respect, his real self begins to emerge without the restrictions of previously learned behavior patterns. As a result of this work, I'm beginning to get some glimmerings of the basic similarities and differences between males and females in terms of their internal needs (the basic human requirements for survival and growth) and processes (the way in which the individual obtains and uses what he gets). We seem to have almost no knowledge of the essence of maleness and femaleness based on the individual's internal world. The problem is a paradox. We are afraid to let go of our external categories and trust our own unique insides to see what emerges, and we cannot begin to get any valid picture of maleness and femaleness until that happens.

Chapter Three:

Sexual Identity Defined: Nurturing and Assertion

I see seven major areas of individual self-expression and need.
In the following three chapters I would like to discuss these
as the basis for defining maleness and femaleness. They are:
nurturing, assertion, building, producing, creating, rhythm,
and connection.

The first and most important need has to do with emotional feeding and nurturing. A child's nurturing needs—
usually met by a female in the child's early years—include
feeding, stroking, encouragement, and validation. Feeding
includes the mother's attention to the child's physical
hunger, plus her expression of love by the gift of herself—her
time and attention and feelings. Stroking implies physical
contact, holding and comforting. Encouragement is both
direct and indirect. Directly, it involves the parent's recognition and expression to the child of the growth aspects of the

child's venture rather than the outcome: i.e., "You took two steps more than you did yesterday," rather than "You didn't make it to the chair." This kind of encouragement requires that the parent see the child as a totally unique organism, constantly growing and changing, rather than a performer or conformer. Indirectly, encouragement involves the parent's giving the child space without judgment to assist the child in expressing and appreciating his own uniqueness.

Let me explain this. I do not believe that a child has to be taught how to be male or female. I believe that a child who is born physically male is also born emotionally male. All the necessary parts are there inside and outside. He is a totally formed small being. He does not need someone to fill up the gaps or give him an identity. True, that identity is embryonic, but it is all there. He is a person from the moment of birth, maybe before. He needs someone who will give him the structure, nurturing, and space to learn to understand, appreciate and define his identity for himself. I do not believe that identity is inherited. I see no reason to assume that a child's personality will be anything like the personality of either parent or of anyone else in his family. I believe this assumption would be evident beyond any doubt if more parents saw their children as separate people rather than as extensions of themselves. Many people spend most of their lifetimes overcoming parental intrusions upon their uniqueness. Often, parents intrude with the best of intentions. They have been culturally educated to believe that the child is totally a reflection of themselves and their ability as parents. This is simply not true. Parents certainly do have tremendous influence on the growth of their children. They can seriously impair a child's functioning by abandoning him or intruding on him. However, it is a two-way street. The child also is a person and makes decisions for himself almost from the moment of birth. Each child has his own unique way of growing and learning. Some children have an innate need to push more, experiment more, do everything the hard way; and it is foolish for a parent to assume he is totally responsible for his child's mistakes. They share a mutual responsibility. It is important for parent and child continually to reassess what belongs to the child, as a result of his unique growth rhythm and pattern, versus what belongs to the family, in terms of some breakdown in the family's ability to provide nurturing, structure, and space for individual differences. All of this implies a totally different way of looking at maleness and femaleness. If you assume that the male infant, for example, is already a total person, then you also assume that everything that comes out of him is male. This view is polarized from what we usually do in our culture, which is to measure and compare everything the child does or expresses against some culturally determined image of what a male or female should be like. However, I believe that true validation, another important aspect of nurturing, is possible only from this framework—accepting what comes out of or from the child as appropriate to who the child is as a small male or female.

With the male child, it is vital that all of the above nurturing needs be met in the framework of separateness from his mother—that nurturing be given without seduction or control on her part. If a mother's own needs for warmth and nurturing are not being met and she is not facing and dealing with this openly, then, she may not separate the warmth and affection she feels in relation to her child from her other needs for warmth which realistically belong in an adult relationship. Subsequently, her relationship with her child takes on a kind of seductive possessiveness—a smothering quality or a coalition between mother and child against father and the rest of the world.

A mother may use her nurturing function to control the child if she feels that her worth is in some way dependent on him—i.e., "If you love me and respond to me, then I am a good person and a good mother." The child is then not a separate person, but an extension of her. Since her self-esteem is dependent on how he behaves, she communicates to him that having a mind of his own is tantamount to betrayal of her. She may communicate this directly—"Why don't you do what I tell you? Don't you love me?" or indirectly by looking hurt, withdrawing, or attacking him in judgmental ways when he rebels or wants to go his own way. A mother who sees her child as a separate person will view his behavior as a statement about himself, not about her, and will handle it as such. She may be furious at what he is saying or doing, but she sees his behavior as an indication that he sees things differently than she does and not as a personal attack on her. Whatever way she chooses to handle his behavior, love is never the issue. The issue is that they see things differently. As the parent, she is in charge and must decide whether to give the child space to go his own way or whether to set and enforce limits. That decision usually rests on the extent to which the child's safety may be involved, how good his judgment is about his abilities, and whether or not he may be infringing on someone else's rights—not on whether he is right or wrong, a good or bad boy.

If a mother meets her son's needs for nurturing without putting strings on her giving, then the child's experience of nurturing and his ability to get it are, to him, forever separate from his autonomy. He does not have to give up his independence in order to receive. If, on the other hand, he has to cut into himself in some way—curtail his assertion, repress his feelings, be someone he isn't—in order for her to love him, then he will connect nurturing with lack of assertion or with manipulation. For example, mother is very loving and giving unless he talks back to her or disagrees with her. If he disobeys, she doesn't just discipline him, she withdraws from him or makes judgments about his worth or his feeling of her. If he wants to get from her, then he must keep his own ideas

to himself and pretend that he thinks and feels the same way *X*
she does. He then gets from her, but feels depreciated in the
process. Later on, he may reject any form of nurturing
altogether, feeling the price is too high; and, in effect, starve
himself emotionally. He may not try to get from people
either, because he learned his lesson well in his early years,
and assumes all nurturing from anyone has such a price, or
because it is too painful for him to try again. Any of these
compromises reduces his potential for deep relationships and
for expression and expansion of his creativity.

When a man learns from his mother that he can receive
nurturing from a woman without strings, without becoming
less of a man, then she has given him the gift of his own full
power, because he is then free to own and honor his needs
and to go after what he wants without fear of loss to himself.
Nurturing is vital to the male; my observation is that the male
uses tremendous energy because of the nature of his assertive
processes (which I'll go into detail about later in this
chapter). Most males operate on 10 or 20 percent of their
real power or they burn themselves out early because of their
inability to drink freely at the fountain. I think the male's
primary source of effective nurturing is the female. He may
get nurturing from solitude, from hunting and fishing, from
poker with the boys—and these outlets are valuable to him,
but poor substitutes for female nurturing if it can be ob-
tained without loss to him.

When a male receives the gift of nurturance from his
mother, he grows into an adult with the ability to trust a
female and to trust himself with a female. He will establish a
lifelong relationship with his mother, not as son to mother,
but as adult to adult; and the relationship will continue to be
a nurturing one. The nature of the nurturance shifts—trust is
the basis of the adult nurturing relationship. The relationship
is nurturing because he doesn't have to use energy to defend
himself or prove himself. He can be who he is without sham

and can rely on her to be honest with him about herself. This process in a mother-son relationship between two very separate people does not interfere with his subsequent husband-wife relationship. On the contrary, it lays the base for his search for women whom he can trust and with whom he can use his energy for creative exploration and building rather than a power struggle. This unique aspect of the mother-son relationship has been widely distorted in our culture into parodies of mother as a divinity or as a castrating bitch.

The reality is that the mother who bestows on her son the gift of his own power by giving to him without taking away from him, establishes a lifelong connection via the power of that gift. The male then learns to experience himself as a warm and loving being. Each relationship he establishes becomes a vehicle for him to experience his own feelings on a deeper and more pervasive level. Thus he grows by each experience and so cannot really lose, no matter what the outcome of the relationship. As he experiences himself as a loving being, he may at times be content just to savor that experience. For example, he may look at his wife or his child or a good friend, and feel a warm rush of feeling. He may just want to relish that feeling, let it flow all through him, see what it feels like to let himself totally love without really doing anything about it at the moment. That process alone, the savoring and total experience of a feeling, produces growth in the individual. If the feeling flows into action, he has many alternative ways to express his warmth—sex is just one way, albeit a very important one. However, he can experience nurturing relationships with many women in his life, and as long as the rules of his marriage, whatever they are, are not broken, these relationships can only enhance his marriage because they deepen his ability to love. In other words, the more you really experience loving feelings, the more you expand and enrich your capacity for love. In our culture, people tend to leap from stimulus to action and miss

22

the whole process so vital to growth—that of experiencing the feeling totally within themselves and letting the action flow from that experience.

There are two aspects to adult nurturing needs—that which the individual gives to himself, and that which he gets from others.

Self-nurturing needs include:

A. The ability to take space when needed. People have varying requirements for privacy and for contact with others. Some people crave occasional periods of silence and aloneness just as they need food and water. The desires for aloneness and space are survival and growth needs, but are not often honored and appreciated as such.

B. A willingness to take good care of oneself physically with adequate exercise, sleep, balanced diet; and enough self-esteem to keep others from interfering or intruding in this area.

C. The ability to establish and maintain boundaries—to say no when you don't want to do something, to say no when you don't want to receive. Giving can sometimes be intrusive even when it's done with the best of intentions. Often we operate as though we should take whatever anyone wants to give because the act of giving should be recognized. How often have you seen someone determined to give what he or she wants to give regardless of what the receiver wants? The reality is that we are not always in a position to take. For example, a husband may want to take his wife out to dinner, something she normally enjoys. However, he may have picked an evening when there is a special program she wants to see on television. It is important that she be able to hold to her boundaries rather than go, and then respond to his gift by feeling deprived because she isn't doing what she really wants to do. It is equally important that he be able to accept her boundaries as an indication of where she is inside of herself at that moment and not as a lack of appreciation for his desire to give to her. In that instance, it is a gift for the husband to respect her limits without making her pay the price of saying no at the expense of hurting his feelings; and it is a gift on her part to be honest about where she is so that he can trust that he won't intrude on her. It is difficult to give to someone you love when you can't be sure that person will let you know what he or she really wants. Also, it is possible to recognize and appreciate someone's intent to give without having to accept the gift.

D. An attitude of understanding. This involves being a "good parent" to oneself. For example, if I do something I'm ashamed of, I begin to explore what is going on inside of me that I would behave in a way that doesn't fit me. Perhaps I hit one of my children and hurt the child. I could judge myself, castigate myself, punish myself with guilt and recriminations. However, that would only further undermine my self-esteem and therefore my ability to function appropriately. I can't change my behavior by dumping ashes on my head. If I want to change my behavior, I have to understand what caused me to behave in a way that doesn't fit me. Obviously, I did something that doesn't fit me or I wouldn't feel so badly. If I begin to explore my insides, I might find out that I'm feeling more pressure that day than I can handle and I'm not taking care of myself. I've stretched myself beyond what I can handle. I'm overtired, emotionally drained, and operating on two cylinders instead of six. Or, there is something getting in my way, throwing me off balance. Perhaps I'm worried about something else and feeling very upset; perhaps I'm not feeling up to par physically. I may not be honoring my limitations, may be expecting myself to do more than I can handle well in that instant. I may need to lower my standards at times or just let some things go. Basically, I need to make room for my limitations without condemning myself for having limitations. Self-nurturing requires that I let go of any external judge as a guide for my behavior, and focus instead on my real needs, capabilities and limitations.

E. Ability to make demands for myself and go after what I need without feeling guilty about it. This ability requires an acceptance on my part that I am basically a worthwhile person, and that if I take care of myself and give to me, I can trust that the best of me will emerge. This is a very different concept than the one which says "Push yourself, drive yourself, crack the whip if you want to produce and be successful!"

F. Reflection. I believe this phenomenon is much more important in the functioning of the female than of the male. It is a process of tuning in on oneself, like a kind of meditation, although it need not be formalized as such. This process requires that the external surroundings be stabilized and soothing. Perhaps I can best define the process with an analogy. I am like a spring of water. As I move and give and work, the spring dwindles to a trickle. When that happens, I need to retreat for a bit into a sheltered place and give the spring a chance to bubble up and flow again; then I can move out once more.

I think there is a decided difference in males and females in this process. Males, when they run dry, are prone to make contact with a female as a way of restoring energy and flow. Females, I believe, need this reflective process and often use contact with males to support it. For example, the female will look to the male to provide the structure that makes it possible for her to go inside herself in this way. The simplest form of this is that she may ask to be cuddled without words or further action. This process of momentarily feeling protected so that she can let go inside of herself is necessary for her to restore her balance. Going inside has to do with getting in touch with one's center—one's inner core of being. The individual uses fantasy, imagery, daydreaming, physical sensation, and sometimes simply a floating state of "being" to facilitate getting in touch with the inner self. The heart of the process is that the mind and body are essentially turned off in terms of activity and goal-directed thought. This experience of staying with oneself in such a state has a balancing, restorative effect. I think that many women—without even being aware of it—use time in the beauty shop, a bubble bath, watching a soap opera or nursing a child to experience this process. I believe that women who have no room or don't allow room for this process, or who don't know how or are afraid to explore themselves in this way, become "strung out"—bitchy, complaining, anxious, and demanding. Males may also use this process as part of their exploration and development of themselves, but I do not think it is connected to their maleness or their sense of themselves as males in any way. In that respect, they can take it or leave it. However, I think this reflective process is central and vital to the female in order for her fully to enjoy her femininity and experience herself as a nurturing female who can give and receive in satisfying ways.

Other-directed nurturing needs involve the search for contact. Many people mistake the external manifestations of contact for the real thing. Stroking, sympathetic listening, verbal support, holding, and sexual expression can be performed between people without any real internal connection. They can also be the outward expression of real internal connection. You can always tell the difference if you are intimately involved with someone and willing to listen to your insides. Contact involves my insides being in touch with your insides—no games, manipulations, or sham. We can be in touch even if both of us are down and not able to give anything concretely. I may be very sad and share my sadness by my words, behavior, physical expression, or tone. You may just hear me or see me and share with me, in the same way, where you are. That may be an equally "down" place. Neither of us is able to reach out to take care of or support the other, but each of us can feel the other there, and loneliness is assuaged by that light touching of each other's insides. I believe everyone has at least a vague longing for that kind of contact. Some people are afraid of it or don't know how to achieve it because they have never experienced it in their lives. The ability to understand, appreciate, and sustain that kind of touch has to be taught. I think the longing for it is innate in all of us.

The female child, for optimal nurturing, needs a mother who is in charge of herself. The mother who has a strong sense of self-worth—who can assert her demands and hold to her boundaries—projects that message about femaleness to her daughter from the very beginning. The mother who does not fully appreciate herself as a female will in some way, even without knowing it, withhold herself or parts of herself from her female child. She is not sure of herself enough to open herself up freely to her girl child because she is afraid she will be an inadequate model of femininity. Very small infants perceive parental withholding and assimilate it as a negative message about themselves—they are not lovable. If a female child has the kind of mother who appreciates herself, then she will receive the nurturing that will lay the base for her understanding and appreciation of the reflective process I described earlier as so necessary to her development as a female. However, her father is the determining factor in the complete formation and later development of that reflective process for the female. In order to sustain the reflective process which is so nurturing to her, the female must learn how to build the structure for herself that protects her and enables her to go into this passive state. It is fine when she connects with a man who can support and enhance that structure or, at times, provide it for her. But, if she is totally dependent on receiving the structure from outside herself, she will be vastly limited in her ability to create and grow when someone else is not available to provide the structure for her. The ability to build this structure for herself is learned in her relationship with her father, from her very early years through adolescence. If he validates her by responding to her and to her sexuality without drawing away, intruding on her, or controlling her, he provides a structure which makes it possible for her to experience and explore herself. It is possible for a father to experience sexual feelings for even a very young daughter, for the simple reason that the human being cannot separate warmth from his or her sexuality. In fact, the greater the man's sensitivity, the more he is apt to perceive his daughter's early beginnings of womanhood and his own responding sexual feelings. If the father translates his sexual feelings as his warmth for his daughter and as his appreciation of her differentness from himself in her developing femininity, then he can accept that he is in charge of his behavior and can direct his warmth in any way he wants. If he responds to his own sexual feelings with fear or guilt, he will not be in charge of his behavior and will distance himself from his daughter by withdrawing physically or emotionally, or by being overly punitive. She perceives that he is in some way afraid of her and translates that as meaning there is something wrong with her.

It is important that the father be aware of and in charge of his own needs for adult warmth and affection so that he doesn't use his daughter as a substitute. If she becomes the only source of emotional satisfaction and meaning for his life, then her growth is inhibited. Instead of focusing on the development of her reflective process and the exploration of who she is, she will feel responsible for him and use much of her energy to take care of him. This, of course, inhibits her letting go of him and making a life of her own when it is appropriate to do so.

When the girl child learns that she can express her warmth, her demands, and her differentness and her father will stand his ground and respond back with his own feelings, then she knows she can connect successfully with a male. That knowledge is vital to her concept of herself as a female. With that knowledge, she is free to honor her needs without fear of loss. She is sure she does not overwhelm men or drive them away. She learns to trust men and to trust herself with men. If she meets men later in her life who do appear to run from her feelings, she knows that withdrawal process belongs to them and to their inability to handle their feelings directly. She can say no when she needs to; she can make demands for space when necessary; she can be comfortable in honoring her own boundaries and asserting her needs. She does not have to prove her femininity by being someone less or different than who she is. She is already sure of herself as a female who can get what she wants by being who she is. Her abilities to set limits, make demands, and assert her needs are the struts of the protective structure she builds around herself when she wants to make space for the tender reflective process. Without this experience, she is constantly searching outside of herself in her adult life for someone to provide a protective structure. She will manipulate males or other fe-males and depreciate herself in order to get it; and that very process undermines the sense of self-worth necessary to be able to tune in and explore the richness of her insides. She may connect with a Big Daddy who will take care of her and protect her as long as she doesn't become too assertive; or find someone who will let her be in control. If she is in control, she is sure of maintaining the relationship since her partner is so dependent on her. The only problem is that it feels like a one-way street to her. She is the one always in charge and taking care of things, which is the price she pays for having a constant obedient servant. Either way, all her energies are directed toward maintaining the structure of the marriage and repressing those parts of herself which might jeopardize the relationship. The process of reflection then becomes frightening because it takes time and energy away from guarding the external structure she has built. In addi-tion, if she really took time to pay attention to her feelings she would be aware of her dissatisfaction with that struc-ture. She has built that external structure of her marriage because she is convinced she must have that relationship to survive and could not manage alone. The irony is that she does not feel a whole person when not in touch with that reflective process; and, she cannot develop the reflective process without a sense of herself as a whole person.

The next area of need and self-expression in males and females has to do with assertion. The assertion process in the male is his primary way of experiencing himself and learning about himself. This process is vital and essential to the male in order for him to feel comfortable and appreciative of himself as a male. By assertion, I do not mean aggression. I mean the extension of himself in trying on feelings, impulses, ideas, and expressions for size. The manner in which he does this may be aggressive, or it may be quiet and unassuming or whatever fits his person. The process is one of constantly extending outside of himself. For example, he has an idea. He will immediately put it into words or action and test it out on someone else. This is not to say that males do not reflect or explore inside of themselves. They do, of course, but the assertion process is inherent to their sense of maleness. Males who are inhibited in asserting, because of their early learning and family experience, do not feel comfortable and secure in their maleness. The male will continue to explore, to experiment, to extend himself out until he feels drained; then he will return to the female for nurturing and refreshing.

The male-female balance then requires an understanding of the differences between males and females in these two vital processes of assertion and nurturance. The female needs to respect and appreciate her reflective process as vital to her ability to sustain her nurturing function. The male needs to appreciate that his ability to honor and respect his nurturing needs is vital to his realization of his potential as a creative male. Each needs to understand that he or she is not dependent on the other to survive and grow, but that each can be greatly enhanced by what the other has to offer that is different and complementary. The male can learn to respect the times when his partner pulls away from him to go into herself. It is an important process to both of them because it is a refueling place for her and not a statement of rejection or disinterest with regard to him. The female can learn to respect the male's need to extend himself as vital to his growth and feeling of self-worth; it is not a statement that he doesn't want to include her and doesn't love her.

The assertion process in the female is her way of testing out, validating or invalidating what she has discovered in her reflective process. What we often laughingly call woman's intuition is a product of the reflective state. Men and women both tend to put down what is really a valuable resource. The intuition is not magical thinking. It consists of ideas, perceptions, mental flashes, thoughts, and feelings that emerge out of the reflective state. The individual then needs to educate herself to the meanings of her intuitive flashes by asserting them and seeing what happens. She is really expanding the use of the perceptual apparatus by this process—educating herself to learn what certain intuitive reactions mean in terms of reality. For example, I wake up in the morning with a fear that I'll have an accident today. Am I really seeing the future or does that feeling mean something else? If I let myself admit it and don't put it down, I can find out. It may be related to the fact that I have decided to return to school after twenty years away from it. I may learn that I have disaster phantasies every time I move into a new growth phase—that's my reaction to something new. Once I understand that process I can handle it with a minimum expenditure of energy, which leaves the bulk of my energy available to handle the new phase of growth.

Many of the female's directions, ideas, and growth impulses will come out of her reflective state, whereas for the male, these come out of the action state. The female may assert, like the male, in whatever manner suits her—aggressive, forceful, quiet, gentle. I don't believe the manner of expressing assertiveness is unique to male or female. When the female explores, via assertion, whatever has emerged from her reflective state, she will then go back into her reflective state. Her process, graphically illustrated, would be an in-and-out flow, like this:⁓⁓⁓. The male's process of assertion will extend out, dwindle abruptly to a low where he will connect for nurturing and restoration, jump to a new stage and continue on:——⌄——

It becomes clear how an understanding of the basic differences in male-female expressiveness could avert much distortion in the male and female's understanding of each other. For example, if he reaches a low at the same time she is at an inward place, neither is getting what he wants and needs from the other. If each can understand that this is because of a basic difference rather than that the other is being stubborn, doesn't care, or is interested in someone else, then adjustments might be made. At least they could both ride through that period with less upheaval or real damage to their relationship. Each might express disappointment, hurt, or irritation, but there would not be recriminations, unrealistic expectations, and depreciative judgments.

Chapter Four:

Sexual Identity Defined: Building, Producing, Creating

There are three areas of need and self-expression which I do not see as different in males and females: building, producing, and creating. However, I do see these areas as dependent on the assertion and nurturing processes for their full development and expression. I believe that the need for creating, producing, and building is universal, but what each of these processes means and how each is expressed is entirely unique to the individual.

I define the building process as that of making a structure—starting with a base, adding additional parts that fit into the base and developing a "whole." The structure may then be modified, enlarged, or even evolve into a totally new structure; but the components (base, parts, whole) are always there. Each step in the building process is related to the last and to the next. This process may be expressed by the individual in the building of a home, a family, a business, a garden, a boat, even model airplanes.

The process of production has to do with the realization of a tangible product—a painting, money, an invention, whatever. These two processes may seem similar. However, within the individual, the structuring is emphasized in the building process, while in the production process the emphasis is on the concrete result. By emphasis, I mean that which gives the individual his sense of satisfaction and feeling of aliveness.

The creative process is the process of taking in information, education, life experience, observations, perceptions, sensations, and responses from others; then, letting it all come together and assimilate inside of you. Out of that assimilation evolves and emerges some way of doing, some way of thinking, some way of being that is uniquely your own creation. I do not know if everyone is creative in this sense. In this culture, it is very difficult to determine, for this kind of creativity is possible only if the individual is in touch with his feelings, knows who he is and is comfortable with that identity. With such wildly creative people as Van Gogh and F. Scott Fitzgerald, I don't know if their creativity was a result of their deep emotional disturbances—in some way an attempt to work out the internal agony—or if it emerged in spite of their disturbances. I do believe that for an individual to sustain a creative flow he has to have a solid base inside himself about who he is. The individual who follows his creative flow will go farther and farther out into pioneer territory where no one else has been. That is at once frightening and exciting. The individual is periodically flooded with intense feelings of excitement, uncertainty, and fear. If he does not have something solid inside him to ground him—a place he can come back to for reassurance—he will burn himself out or he will begin to use external means to squelch the intensity of his feelings which at times becomes unbearable. Excitement, like other pleasurable experiences such as tickling or stroking, can become irritating or even painful if prolonged. Historically, the use of drugs, alcohol, and hedonistic pursuits have been common among people whose life function has been focused around creating from raw material inside of themselves.

My experience has been that each individual, if not blocked in some way by his life experience, will focus his major life functioning around one of these three processes —building, producing, or creating—depending upon which makes him or her feel most alive. I do not believe that any activity in and of itself is a creative, building, or producing activity. It depends on how the activity connects with the individual's insides. Making a home and raising children may be intensely creative for some women and nothing but a drab chore to others. One person may throw an organization together in a haphazard way—another will build it. In our culture, we have confused and misinformed ourselves by labeling certain activities and vocations creative—like homemaking, child rearing, art, medicine. I have seen many would-be artists who are so rigidly constrained in their approach to their work that they are totally out of touch with any creative flow. The secret is for the individual to explore what process makes him feel most alive, then continue to fit the process and the activity to that feeling of aliveness. The feeling of aliveness I can best describe as being turned on, experiencing an unblocked flow of energy within oneself, a supra-awareness to stimuli, a quality of letting go into the moment with an ability to experience the moment totally.

Chapter Five:

Sexual Identity Defined: Rhythm and Connection

The next area of expression has to do with rhythm. An understanding of his individual rhythm is basic to a person's development of a sense of aliveness and of his own unique identity. Rhythm is innate, but it is not inherited. It is the organism's natural flow. You can observe it most clearly in a newborn infant. Each infant has his own unique pattern for eating, sleeping, sucking and for physical contact with adults. He has his own way of reaching out for what he wants and his own way of setting limits or pulling back from situations or people. If his rhythm is ignored or intruded on, he will get upset. If you watch him carefully, you can see the rhythmic pattern emerge. As he grows older, that pattern will become more pronounced and will show in everything he does—the way he grows, the way he meets new situations, how he handles frustration, how he approaches learning something new, how he reaches out for contact with others, when he wants to be by himself, and his sexual cycle. His rhythm is evident in his expression of himself in all the areas I've discussed—nurturing, asserting, building, producing, creating. It is also a vital part of the male-female relationship which I'll discuss in detail in Chapter Ten.

Unfortunately, most of us are not taught to tune into and appreciate our natural rhythms. Our parents and the extended culture are more apt to thwart our natural rhythms by their expectations and standards. I think this must account for the expression about fitting a round peg into a square hole. It takes more energy to force ourselves into ways of operating that don't fit our rhythms. Therefore, we may have only a small amount left for use in our growth and development in comparison to the potential energy resources actually available. For example, the reflective state I described earlier could appear, by our cultural standards, to be a lazy, unproductive, useless state. In reality, it is a state of being in which the head is temporarily turned off—we are not figuring, planning, thinking, or conceptualizing. However, our perceptual, sensorial, and physical apparatus may be digesting and assimilating all kinds of data not yet transmitted into thought or action. Have you noticed that an infant, just before bursting into some new growth phase, will often appear to regress slightly? For example, a child has been sitting up, crawling, and pulling himself up on his feet for some time. Then, for a day or so, maybe even a week or two, he will seem disinterested in doing anything. He may sleep more or seem restless and irritable. Suddenly, you look, and he is up and walking. I believe that each of us has a kind of "preparation" place for each new growth phase in our lives. However, we tend to put negative labels on these preparation places because we do not understand them as basic to our natural growth rhythms. My preparation place is a state of lethargy, decreased energy, and some immobilization. If there is nothing wrong with me physically and no trauma in my life, then I know my insides are getting ready to move into a new stage of growth for me. This state may last as long as three or four months, and will end suddenly with a burst of energy, ideas, and new enthusiasm. I seem to catapult myself effortlessly into a new place. Someone else's preparation state may be characterized by anxiety, or a low mood which could be misinterpreted as depression, or irritability with no evident cause. I am sure that this state is different for everyone and probably vastly misunderstood by almost everyone. Therefore, most people, rather than protect this state and allow themselves to flow out of it naturally, will push themselves out of it by activity, denial, depreciation, or even medication. Thus, they lose adequate preparation or delay growth altogether for the time. The human organism, however, must grow or die; so, if the individual fights his growth process, he may develop some physical or emotional illness that will literally force him to pay attention to himself.

I believe that our whole educational system is built on frustrating our natural growth rhythms rather than on teaching us to learn to flow with those rhythms. This stems from the old Puritan principles of growth—push, drive yourself hard, keep your nose to the grindstone, crack the whip on yourself or you'll never amount to anything. The basic underlying philosophy behind this concept is that people are really no good, that we will not grow, produce, or accomplish unless we force ourselves to do so. The acceptance of rhythm is based on a polarized concept—that each human organism is a unique energy system whose life-force is constantly toward growth. Maximum growth potential can be realized automatically by fitting the environment and all its forms of education—parental guidance, formal education, community responsibility and compatibility—to the natural rhythm of the energy system. The underlying philosophy of this concept is respect for the individual's autonomy and executive. Most of the time the individual does know what is best for him, even from birth. He may err in judgment at times for lack of experience or knowledge, but this is usually in the areas of learning new skills and social responsibility. In the ways he chooses to learn, how he needs to experiment, what he needs in the way of limits and space, each of us knows what he needs in order to grow. We will make that clear from our very first day if others will only pay attention.

The final area of expression is that of connection with other people. The process of connecting is different in male and female in some aspects and similar in others. The male connects primarily for direct nurturing in the form of giving and receiving. The female connects primarily for nurturing via structure. A man wants a woman who will give to him without strings; and, a woman wants a man who will stand firm in the face of her assertions and respond with his own feelings without overreacting by withdrawing or attacking her. I think that the ways males and females go about connecting might not be so different except for serious cultural distortions. For example, the accepted standards that males are the sexual aggressors in male-female relationships and that women always want marriage and trap men into it, are confusing fallacies for both sexes. The monogamous relationship fits some, but not all men and women. Some people do better in a commune-type living arrangement. Others prefer a series of relationships, monogamous in nature, but with a periodic change of partner. Still others might do better with more than one relationship at a time, in varying depth. I believe the relationship that fits the individual depends on where he wants to focus his energies. The monogamous relationship holds the potential for tremendous excitement and aliveness if both individuals involved are willing to take the risk to grow and invest time and energy. Not everyone really wants to do this—some people would rather invest that energy elsewhere. A man or woman might want a less stimulating relationship at home to complement a very stimulating work situation. Some people want excitement in every area of their lives and will invest deeply in a marriage as well as in a vocation and perhaps also in an avocation, depending on how much energy is available to the individual. I believe the energy capacity varies widely in individuals. The important thing is that most people, unless too frightened or emotionally disturbed by their life experiences, will invest their energy in whatever makes them feel most alive.

I do not believe that the type of connection the individual makes is different for males and females. I think that choice is sex-linked in our culture because the monogamous family unit has been our only way of rearing children. However, if our society had different ways of rearing children which gave parents more community support and more choices, then I think women would be no different than men in being open to a variety of choices about the kind of relationships most fitting to them.

I feel that the need for connection is equally vital in both males and females. Individuals grow in two concurrent areas of development: One is in the area of self-exploration which the female accomplishes primarily through the reflective process and the male achieves through the assertion route (discussed earlier); the other growth area is through connection with others.

The response and validation of others encourages us to touch deeper parts of ourselves. The infant, when he is hungry for contact—or when someone tickles him, holds him, or loves him—responds with his whole body. He reaches out with arms, legs, and a smiling face—everything moves with the same message—he is pleased and wanting more. That process of feeling a feeling with one's total being will automatically move the individual in a growth direction. When the individual is joyous and lets himself savor that joy before he goes into action, the savoring process will put him in touch with parts of himself he had not been aware of before. For example, a friend of mine moves to another part of the country and that makes me feel sad. I sit in a dejected position—slumped, with my head down—and just experience that sadness. My head, my chest, and my arms and legs feel heavy. My gut feels nothing. I picture and experience that nothingness as a blank space. I do not push myself—I just let myself sink into that heaviness and experience what the blank space feels like to me. I get a feeling of anxiety in my gut—a little gnawing sensation. I let myself sink into that sensation and tears come to my eyes, I let go into the crying and begin to sob for several minutes. As I am crying, I realize that friend was very important to me. I depended on her for many things and I shall miss her greatly. As I am crying, I experience my yearning for our old friendship, my anger at her for leaving and my sadness at my loss. At the same time, I experience that I want her to do what is best for her and I'm glad she is happy about the move. I let myself move back and forth among all these feelings and gradually a kind of calmness seeps through me. Then, I realize that I said goodbye to her earlier with words, but not with all my feelings. As I have gone through this process, I have completed that transaction of letting go of her as far as our past relationship was concerned. Now I can go on to form a different kind of connection with her, restricted by distance, and to find a similar kind of close friendship here with someone else. I have no leftover, unresolved feelings to get in the way of my knowing what I want and going after it.

If the individual learns this savoring process, his growth will be enhanced by other people's responses to the way he manifests himself and by the stimulus of their feelings for him. Unfortunately, most of us as we grow up do not continue to develop and appreciate the savoring process. We tend to jump from stimulus into action with nothing in between. For example, a man and a woman feel warmly toward each other. In our society, if they are not prepared to act on that warmth sexually, then they usually repress it or deny it, because we live with the assumption that if you feel something you have to act on it. That assumption makes for tremendous waste. If each could savor what it feels like to him or her to feel warm all over, and could linger over and hoard the feeling like lazing in a warm pool or relishing a good meal, then each would grow simply by the experience of self as a warm, loving person. Whatever action was fitting would simply flow out of that experience easily, without force. They might just smile, touch, hug, express the warmth verbally, have a sexual experience or just share the glow of that moment—whatever behavior might fit the moment and who they are. Even if the other person did not respond with comparable feeling, the one who felt the warmth could still have the experience of himself as a loving person. That experience would enhance his growth regardless of the outcome of the relationship. With an understanding of this process, the individual begins to learn that even if he does not get everything he wants in every relationship, he gets something important each time he lets himself get involved and feel. Once he understands he cannot really lose, he will be able to risk himself more freely and thus not miss out on the best that life has to offer—the opportunity to feel deeply and richly, which is the essence of being alive.

In order for the individual to experience this kind of growth through his relationships with others, connections must be made out of separateness. Real connections are possible only if each person is aware of himself as a whole, autonomous individual who is dependent on himself for emotional survival. Such a person takes full responsibility in a relationship for whether or not he is satisfied, happy, unhappy, pleased, or desirous of change. He does not make the other person responsible for his life or his well-being. When I refer to emotional survival, I mean that the individual needs the sure awareness within himself that he can manage alone. He may not want to be alone, and he may be very unhappy in that state; but he knows deep inside himself that he will not die or fall apart if he is alone. If he does not have that knowledge and, instead, feels that without his partner he cannot function, then he will not be totally himself in that relationship. He will change his behavior to please the other, give what he does not really want to give and repress feelings he thinks will be unacceptable to his partner. With such masking and withholding of feelings, it is impossible to tell who he really is. In this kind of relationship, where both partners are dependent on each other in this way, they build up a whole set of external rules for behavior which keeps everything nice and doesn't rock the boat. They build a cozy structure which may work for awhile as long as neither of them has to pay too high a price to maintain it. However, they lose the possibility of ever really knowing about each other and themselves and of growing with each other.

It is very common in the male-female relationship for each to blame the other if needs are not being met. The blaming response is based on the infantile assumption that "the world owes me a living." Some people miserably cling to that assumption until death; but, it is a lethal assumption which prevents growth. It produces resentment, inertia, and destruction in a relationship—the play *Who's Afraid of Virginia Woolf* exemplifies this process beautifully. As an example, if a husband makes a request of his wife and she understands his request, but does not give, then the husband assumes that although there is nothing wrong with what he is asking, it may not fit her to comply. She may not be able to or she may not want to or she may not feel like it at the moment. The husband then takes responsibility for getting what he wants somewhere else, or for dealing with feelings generated by the lack of response. He may let her know he feels angry

46

or hurt, but he doesn't beat her over the head as though she were deliberately withholding out of some desire to hurt him. He assumes she is withholding out of difference—she is not in a place inside of herself to give, or she cannot give what he wants without hurting herself in some way. For example, a man may communicate very clearly to a woman that he is interested in a sexual experience. She may communicate equally clearly that she is not; not because of the way he approached her or something he hasn't done, but because of where she is inside herself at the moment. He understands her response and it may disappoint or irritate him, but he doesn't perceive it as a statement about himself or their relationship—whether or not he is an attractive male or whether she loves him—but simply a statement about her and where she is inside, separate from him. He then accepts that and takes responsibility for himself. He may choose to go elsewhere for sex, unless that would jeopardize the relationship and his investment is such that he does not want to do that. He may do something else that is pleasurable for him; or, he may stay with his irritation and disappointment until something emerges from inside of himself as a way to deal with those feelings. He may learn something about himself by staying with his disappointment and experiencing what that feels like to him. He may recall memories of other times when he has felt sad or alone—memories he had long forgotten. Some of these might be unpleasant and some very pleasant, but each tells him more about himself and who he is as a total person.

The processes for maintaining and sustaining a relationship connection are different in males and females. The female likes to keep in close touch—perhaps in varying depth at different times—but she uses the relationship like a touchstone to help her restore her balance. If she becomes emotionally drained, overtired or overburdened she will turn to her husband either directly, by communicating her weary or up-tight feelings, or indirectly by complaining or getting panicky. At these moments, she doesn't want advice, direction, criticism, or a takeover from her husband. She wants a solid response about how he feels at that moment in relation to her. It often doesn't make too much difference to her what the feeling is. He may feel irritated, sympathetic, bored, or upset. He may even say he doesn't know what he feels and wants space to see where he is inside. What is important to her is that he responds to her with whatever his insides are at the moment, and that she can count on his doing that. That process gives her a sense of solidarity in the relationship that has a balancing effect for her.

To the female, the male will periodically seem distant and out of touch with her when he is absorbed in his assertion process. His process in this respect is often misinterpreted by the female because it is so different from hers. He will move in deeply into the relationship, then move away from it and repeat this over and over. The relationship is like an elastic band to him and some men will stretch it very far. I think there is considerable variety in the degree, time and length of stretch in different males, but the basic process is the same. Therefore he needs space in the relationship, at least in the sense that the female does not judge him to be bad, wrong, or uncaring because his manner of connecting is somewhat different than hers. If both partners understand each other's needs in this respect as basic to who they are as male and female and not some unreasonable demand on the part of each, they may be able to accommodate each other without a significant loss to either individually. She may be able to allow him more room if she knows he needs it for his own growth and self-satisfaction—the better he feels about himself the more she will get from him. He may be able to shorten his stretch somewhat without any real loss to his growth process if he knows that this contribution to her balance will mean better nurturing from her to him.

Another, very subtle, difference between males and females occurs as a result of their being very close and giving with each other. When the male experiences a sense of fulfillment and joy, he wants to expand. He loves the whole world and everyone in it, is apt to express his joys in ways that go outside the relationship—kidding with waitresses, dancing with chorus girls, inviting friends over, having a drink with the boys, making big plans for his work. He is not really avoiding or depreciating the relationship. He is figuratively beating his chest. I believe that this is a quality in males frequently misunderstood and unappreciated by females. It is a kind of cockiness which you can best observe in boys three to five years old. I think that, unless it is repressed by a male's parents, this quality is always an important aspect of maleness. It comes out in very different ways according to the particular male personality, but there is a quality of "look at me!" in the behavior. Females often feel embarrassed or threatened by this aspect of the male personality because they don't experience it themselves; therefore they feel left out and alone when the male is expressing this part of himself.

The female, after an experience of intimate joy, wants to stay in a kind of quiet contact with the male, feeling that he is there but not necessarily interacting with him in any way. She just wants to savor the warmth together. She likes to relive and marvel over the experience. This process is often misunderstood by the male because he doesn't feel the need for this, doesn't understand it, and tends to interpret it as a demand from the female for more, which makes him anxious. Men and women may be able to give space and support to these differences between them if they understand that by doing so, they are deepening each other's sense of maleness or femaleness. That process of adding to each other's sense of self as a sexual being produces tremendous rewards in the relationship. These rewards may more than atone for the anxiety they may feel momentarily when their differentness shows acutely.

There is another vital and equally subtle difference between males and females in the manner of connecting with each other. Basically, the male-female connection works best when the male takes the lead in saying what he feels, what he thinks, and what he wants and doesn't want. It isn't a matter of making decisions for the female, being the boss, or taking over for her in any way; it has to do with freely declaring where he is inside of himself. I think this manner of relating is natural to the male if it isn't educated out of him at an early age. I think it is the nature of the male to quickly risk coming out with where he is if he hasn't been taught in his growing up experience that this is dangerous or hurtful. If he experiences such expression as hurtful to him, then he learns to withhold and keep his feelings to himself. Such withholding is extremely destructive to him and his sense of himself as a male because it violates his natural assertion process.

The male's willingness to declare himself supports the female's need for a protective structure. This doesn't mean she is less assertive than the male. It has more to do with the interactional pattern of assertion. She will often look to the male to see where he is and use his declaration as her touchstone to get in touch with her reflective process. Then she will offer her feelings and thoughts out of that reflective process which will serve as a balance for him. The interaction will work the other way around also, but basically it follows this pattern. There is a delicate balance established out of this complementarity that is rewarding and enhancing to both. The balance is delicate as both must be able to respect and appreciate what the other has to offer without feeling depreciated because each is benefiting by something the other does better or differently. For example, the female might feel she should be more impulsive or the male that he should be more reflective. If I see you, husband, express yourself more quickly or clearly than I, then I feel something is wrong with me rather than appreciate your assistance. In this instance, she sees their differentness as a threat rather than an advantage. The differences between males and females can lead to excitement and enhancement and, also, moments of separateness and aloneness. All of these experiences are part of the whole package. If you strive to be more alike, you may have fewer moments of feeling separate and thus have less anxiety, but you also dissipate the excitement. There is nothing wrong with that necessarily; it is simply a matter of "pay your money and take your choice!"

Another difference in the way males and females connect has to do with the way each uses sexual contact as a way of expression. Males experience sexual contact as part of the whole nurturing experience with females. Therefore, a male may express many feelings besides love and warmth in the sexual relationship. He may have had a very difficult workday and seek sexual contact out of his feelings of frustration and discouragement. His desire for sexual contact may flow out of a sense of loss and sadness in some other area of his life; or he may have a sense of accomplishment and seek contact out of a sense of pleasure and completion. None of these experiences may have anything to do with his relationship with his wife directly. He comes to her with feelings connected to another part of his world which he expresses in his sexual contact with her. The female, on the other hand, seeks out sexual contact primarily out of the flow of where she is in the relationship with her partner at the moment. If she is feeling warm, close, appreciative and appreciated, she responds sexually. Frequently, she will initiate sexual contact following some kind of confrontation in which the male has offered the structure (which I discussed earlier) she desires via the sharing of his deepest feelings with her. The female often experiences her most passionate sexual arousal after the

51

expression and resolution of angry feelings between herself and her partner. By resolution, I do not necessarily mean agreement or compromise. I mean that all of the feelings have been expressed with nothing held back. Neither partner experienced the other falling apart; neither felt put down·or attacked. They each said what they felt and they heard each other out. The male is often confused by the female's seemingly sudden sexual arousal after this kind of set-to. Many misconceptions have grown out of this phenomenon—i.e., the caveman myth that women like to be taken by force, the sado-masochistic love match in which women appear to like to be slapped around, the assumption that women are little girls who want big strong men to take care of them by making decisions for them and taking responsibility off them, the more subtle myth of the man as the strong, silent, stiff-upper-lip type protecting his hysterical mate with his stoicism. The reality is that women do not like to be subdued by force. This is a degrading and depreciative maneuver. However, for the female to experience the full richness of her femininity, she needs the experience of letting go with the full power of her feelings with her partner and being met by him on that level.

For example:

She: I'm furious with you for embarrassing me at that party tonight.
He: I don't understand what you're talking about.
She: You know damn well what I'm talking about and I don't like that smug look on your face either!
He: Now look! I'm getting tired of your slurs; I don't know what you're referring to. If you want to tell me, I'll listen. If you're going to keep sniping at me, I'm going to bed.
She: You bowed and scraped over Marie all evening. I felt like a fool—everyone noticed.

He: I like Marie. What harm does it do if I'm nice to her?

She: You don't love me—I hate you—I hate you—why don't you care about how I feel?

He: What do you mean, I don't care how you feel? I'm involved in this ridiculous argument, aren't I? Of course, I care how you feel, but I'm beginning to feel pretty shit on right now!

She: That's what I mean—I felt shit on when you were fawning over Marie—left out, unimportant—I really felt hurt . . .

He: Look—I'm really sorry you feel hurt—you're very important to me and I don't like for you to feel that way. However, I'm not going to change who I am to make you feel good. I respect your feelings but I don't think my behavior with Marie was out of line at all. Mixing it up with people, including attractive women is my nature—that's the way I am. I don't think I could change that without trying to be somebody else. I won't do that no matter how much I love you.

She: I don't want you to be somebody else. Your charm is part of why I married you. I just didn't know you'd keep spreading it around . . .

He: Well, now you know. My God, it's right out there in front of the world and everybody—it isn't as though I'm having some affair or orgy.

In this dialogue, the husband heard what his wife was feeling. He did not make judgments about her—that she was stupid, wrong, bad. He did not walk out on her, threaten her or try to manipulate her. Neither did he in any way depreciate himself or deny his own feelings. He let her know that he cared about her and wanted to please her, but could not do so in this instance without hurting himself. He then took responsibility for his limits and took a stand about what he could and could not do. His ability to do this is vital to the female. She really does not want to be able to manipulate him. If she can manipulate him simply by coming out strongly with how she feels, then she cannot rely on him. When the male respects himself enough to be clear about his limitations, without apology, then the female feels respect for him and feels protected by him. It is very hurtful to a female's sense of herself as a woman to be able to mow a man down. It is equally destructive for her to be treated like a child, attacked as though she were a bitch or monster, or ignored. She feels deeply appreciative and loving toward a male who can allow her to be totally herself without experiencing that as a loss to himself in some way. For the female this process is the base for the male-female connection. She feels and communicates on many levels that she has a "real male" when she has a man who can do this. The base for the male is his being able to get nurturing from the female without strings. He also feels and communicates on many levels that he has a "real woman" when he has one who gives to him in this way. Those two processes put male and female in greatest awareness of their maleness and femaleness in relation to each other. What is more exciting or rewarding to any of us than that kind of validation from our lovers? The male and female who continually enhance each other's sexuality by these processes are in the laps of the gods.

Chapter Six:

Distortions in Learning

This book is about the essence of maleness and femaleness and the nature of the male-female connection—not a treatise on therapy. However, I don't want to leave anyone with the assumption that he is forever lost if he does not have the base and understanding for the processes I have described in the previous chapter. Therapy is one avenue by which distortions in learning can be corrected and new growth processes taught.

The goal of therapy is not to change the individual—that isn't necessary. One goal is to enable the individual to change the way in which he manifests himself so that his outsides are congruent with his insides. Then he can express who he is spontaneously, congruently, and clearly. The other major goal is to teach the individual how to connect with others in ways that are enhancing and enriching without a loss to his self-esteem. In order for these goals to be accomplished, the individual may have to recognize and let go of many distortions that he learned about expressing himself and connecting with others during his growing-up period. These are now getting in his way and defeating him in getting what he wants in his adult life. He may have learned in his experience with his parents that if you want to be loved and stay out of trouble, you don't come out with how you feel. You adopt some structure for manifesting yourself that you have been taught or that you have evolved out of your own trial and error experience in the family. The structure may be quite foreign to who the child really is but his experience has led him to believe it is necessary for the maintenance of connections to others and for reception of the approval he deems vital to his survival.

A. The Should Structure. The author of the should structure is the judgmental parent. The child perceives that he can maintain a relationship with that parent only by adhering to a rigid code which determines how he should behave and, more important, how he should feel. If he adheres to this code, he is responsible, mature, reliable, good, and acceptable. If he does not honor the code, he is bad, sick, stupid, or crazy. By the time he reaches adulthood, the should structure may be grating, but it is secure and safe. As long as the individual sticks to that structure, he is above criticism and can be sure that society will, if not smile upon him, at least not attack him. Now, there may be nothing negative necessarily in the qualities he is exhibiting. The problem is that they may or may not fit what is really inside him. Often he does not honestly know who he really is and how he really feels about all the virtues he extols. He may even believe that the structure is actually his, instead of superimposed on him by the parent whom he is still (figuratively) carrying around inside of himself. If he does realize the structure does not fit him, he may pay the price to continue with it rather than risk moving away from it because he is so unaware of his own insides that he assumes there is nothing there. Without his should structure, he feels as though he is a big, empty space.

B. **The Paranoid Structure.** The basis of the paranoid structure is emotional deprivation. The child perceives early in his development that his external world (parents, primarily) is unresponsive to his needs and perhaps even hurtful if he reveals vulnerability. Therefore, he believes his survival is dependent on his being able to disguise his real feelings and manipulate the environment around him in such a way that his needs are met without his having to take responsibility for those needs. Almost any kind of manipulation can be rationalized because he perceives the world as hostile and dangerous; therefore, they deserve anything they get. His repertoire of manipulative methods may be endless depending on his intelligence and sensitivity. They may include helplessness, blame, martyrdom, pseudo niceness, seduction, intimidation, reasonableness, and more vicious manifestations such as deliberate lying, stealing, and verbal or physical attack. To consider giving up this structure is terrifying because the individual believes he will be destroyed. If he begins to consider that the world might not be so hostile and some people really do want to give to him, then he feels overwhelmed with guilt at all the things he has done, and his self-esteem becomes jeopardized. He sees his alternatives as continuing with his structure or feeling like some kind of monster.

C. **The Fragmented or Compartmentalized Structure.** The child perceives the outside world (his parents) as unreliable and unpredictable. Therefore, he believes his survival to be dependent on his ability to please, to accurately perceive and adjust to any shifts in the expectations of his parents. As an adult, he continues that structure as an effective means of survival, based on his continuing perception of himself as a weak, ineffective, helpless victim. Therefore, his boss or wife or whoever else is important to him becomes parent surrogate in terms of his structure and his whole external manifestation of himself may change completely depending on whom he is with, where he is, and whether or not he deems the place or people as connected to his survival. Without this structure, the individual sees himself as helpless and abandoned.

D. The Messianic Structure. The child perceives his external world (parents or other survival figures) as caring and reliable, but ineffective; and he believes that he must fill the gaps his parents have or hold them together, or in some way support the parental framework so that his needs can be met and he will survive. He believes his survival is dependent on his being in charge, in control and strong. This is the easiest structure to shift because the individual is usually aware of who he is and in touch with his feelings. At first, he simply feels no one could respond to his "weak" feelings and, in fact, these feelings might rock the boat, so he does not express them. Later, the secondary gains are often so large to the "great white father" types, that they continue the structure of self-aggrandizement. The price is isolation, however, and once the individual sees his dilemma, he is often eager to give it up.

The individual adopts one of these structures to protect himself, minimize his anxiety and to get what he needs because he is convinced his real self will not accomplish any of these things. Therefore, you act "good" and you do all the "right" things and in that way you survive and win approval. Or you withdraw, and as long as you don't cause any trouble, you don't get hurt. Perhaps you learn to manipulate because if you come out directly with your feelings, you are misunderstood or clobbered. Unfortunately, these ways of operating may be successful in helping children through certain types of difficult family situations, but they don't work very satisfactorily for adults, because all these ways of operating are depreciating to the individual. It is as though the person is saying "I can't get what I want by being who I am—I have to pretend to be someone else in order to please, to get for myself, to be accepted." Therefore, the individual must first face that the ways he learned no longer work for him and he must give them up. That is difficult because although the old ways may not work, at least they are familiar. New ways that fit him better have to evolve out of his exploration of who he is, how he really feels and how he can express that feeling in ways appropriate to his unique self.

Therapy deals primarily with four of the growth processes—nurturing, assertion, connection, and rhythm. The therapy experience is too complicated to deal with in brief and would comprise a book in itself. What I want to emphasize is that it is never too late for the individual to get into a positive growth direction. When people come for therapy, they frequently give the message that they feel they have "holes" in them—parts missing because of negative life experiences. I have not found that to be so. The parts may be somewhat damaged or buried, but they are all there. It is a matter of breaking down the barriers in the way to the individual's awareness of his real self and his basic rhythm and then assisting him in building a structure inside of himself—new ways of operating, new ways of thinking and feeling about himself and others—that enables him to experience himself as a solid, whole person. In therapy, growth processes must be taught on two levels—the development of personal self-esteem and the connective level—just as natural growth takes place. The therapy method must fit and follow the individual's natural growth process, rather than force the individual to fit into some particular therapy method. Therefore, I think the best therapists have a repertoire of many methods and techniques which can be applied according to the natural growth rhythm of the individual. In therapy, I teach females how to let go of their frantic search for validation from a male and begin to get in touch with their inner resources, which they have assumed were not there only because they never felt secure enough to explore them. Then the female is able to form a relationship with a male based on a desire for fulfillment and enrichment rather than a need to be rescued or judged. I teach males to own their nurturing needs as connected to their power rather than to weakness and how to get nurturing without loss to themselves. Then a male is free to connect with a female who is equal to him rather than one who may be less exciting but also less threatening.

When the individual (who had lived with one of the structures I discussed earlier) makes a commitment to growth for himself, then he will transfer his survival to the therapist and use the therapist as a bridge. The bridge is necessary because he must let go of the old structure before he has anything new to take its place. On a feeling level, this experience is often perceived as death. The individual may be aware of intense depression, internal chaos, lack of control, perhaps even an experience he will label as "crazy." He has to go through this experience and know he can survive it in order to develop the sense of aloneness as wholeness rather than as death. The bridge, which makes it possible for him to go through this experience and use it for growth, is his experience of a clear, congruent message from the therapist that—"I believe that if you make room for all parts of you, what you will discover will, when put together, be better than anything you could manufacture or superimpose on yourself from the outside." Once the experience of the death of the old structure is complete, and the individual finds he is still there and not destroyed, then begins the process of building the new structure based on his own feelings, rhythm, and growth needs. This process is based on assertion; and it is necessary in the beginning to enable the individual to distinguish assertion from what he may perceive as aggression, selfishness, immorality, or rule breaking. This distinction is taught by enabling the individual to get in touch with the growth intent inherent in his feelings (i.e., desire for contact, for space, for support, recognition, and desire for acceptance of his limitations on the part of others) and to express that intent in ways that fit who he is. He must understand that in the process of learning what fits him, he may make many mistakes and appear quite different from who he really is. For example, if someone has never been able to express anger, his first attempts to do it may be awkward, inappropriate, or somewhat destructive. He then has to learn to assess his assertive attempts on the basis of whether or not they fit his insides rather than whether they were right or wrong or successful. The individual develops his own processes for asserting his feelings, for receiving responses from others about his assertions and for evaluating those responses. He then takes this evaluation plus his own experience and uses the resulting knowledge from this total experience to build a structure on his insides which tells him who he is, how he needs to behave and in what directions he needs to go. Such a structure does not repress or curtail him, but instead gives a sense of solidarity inside. That sense of solidarity gives him the freedom to explore and grow and risk himself. At this point, his survival shifts to himself, and the therapist becomes a friend and an equal.

Chapter Seven:

Variations in the Male-Female Connecting Process

There are many people who do not seek deep intimacy in the male-female connection. I would like to discuss them in relation to the seven areas of individual self-expression that I discussed earlier. For example:

A. Homosexuality. I consider the homosexual or lesbian as the individual who has chosen to make his deep and meaningful nurturing connections entirely with people of the same sex. I have observed that the individual who has chosen to make his or her deep connections with people of the same sex as a way of life, is one who has not developed his ability to assert his deep feelings and connect on that level with people of the opposite sex. I will focus on homosexuality for purposes of clarification here, but lesbianism is included under that framework. These people do not have adult peer relationships with people of the opposite sex in which there is any element of real trust in revealing their deepest feelings of hurt, anger, tenderness, and warmth. Their relationships with people of the opposite sex are guarded and superficial almost as though the opposite sex doesn't really exist in the world. The homosexual represses much or most of his inside feelings in his heterosexual relationships. I am not talking about people who have homosexual experiences sexually. I do not know what is fitting to the biological organism of man in his sexual behavior. Perhaps, as I said earlier, the organism is bisexual and without our strong cultural taboos and biases we might express ourselves freely sexually with both sexes. However, I do know that the unfettered human being has deep, open, committed connections emotionally to both sexes. He or she can and does really love both men and women.

There are many strong homosexual connections where no sexual behavior is involved at all and even where both people may be involved heterosexually. I am referring to the homosexual connection as homosexual because this is where the individual feels free to be himself openly, and therefore where his deep investment is. Again, in these situations, he or she is not freely open with people of the opposite sex, but is defensive, wary, guarded, and closed. These are people whose very early life's experience taught them that people of the opposite sex are not trustworthy—they abandon you, hurt you, or are destructive to you in some important way. Or there has been an absence of meaningful connections in their growth experience with people of the opposite sex, so that they took their warmth where it was most easily found, and have been afraid to reach out and risk new kinds of experience. Therefore, there are gross distortions in both their connection and nurturing growth processes. These people may develop their creative, building, and producing processes in the areas of concrete, tangible outcomes where they can extend outside of themselves as in music, art, architecture. However, they are limited in the areas of communication and human development from achieving their potential because there are parts of themselves they are withholding, denying, or simply do not know about. Their rhythm process is also interfered with in this basically heterosexual world. The constant withholding and withdrawing interferes with a natural rhythmic flow. Because they must pull back in confrontations with the opposite sex, they may frequently create their own world as a subculture within society. Since they do allow themselves to give and accept nurturing, they can, however, often achieve much in areas not dependent on relationships. However, I do not believe these people can realize their overall potential because they are so fragmented. By fragmented, I mean that the homosexual individual appears to be a different person depending on where he is and with whom he is associating. He is functioning as though he has many different identities. This means he may appear to be many different people in the course of a day. He is operating according to the appropriate role function depending on where he is and what he is doing. That kind of constant shifting must take its toll in energy consumption that could otherwise be put to use for growth and creativity. In order to have maximum use and control of his energy, the individual must operate as an integrated, whole organism. This means he is who he is no matter where he is; and he does not change his insides or his outsides to fit the situation or the other people involved. He is not tying up energy hiding how he feels, pretending to feel something else, or avoiding being criticized, judged or otherwise attacked.

B. Asexuality. The individual who does not make deep connections with either males or females is the loner who has never learned how to develop his nurturing process—giving and receiving—or who was so hurt in his attempts to get

65

nurturing for himself in his growing-up experience, that he has just given up. This individual may marry or become otherwise involved with others, but he does not give of himself or allow himself to take. He may give in terms of advice, direction, and money, but not of his insides. Because of this, I believe he is the victim of emotional starvation which cuts drastically into his realization of his potential as a human being. All of his processes are interfered with or underdeveloped without nurturing. His connections are based on external functioning—everyone has his or her role—and are devoid of real give and take. Reflection is the only part of the nurturing process open to him and, without deep connections to validate and test out the reflections or to replenish the individual, he or she burns out early. I believe that if all seven of the processes I have discussed are not inhibited in the individual, but are developed to provide unlimited room for expansion and growth, the individual will continue to grow until he dies. The energy system, I believe, is unlike the physical body in that it is ageless and does not deteriorate unless the individual blocks its flow by the way he sees life and the way he functions.

C. Immature Sexuality. The individual who is infantile in his sexual identity is one who has been inadequately nurtured as a child in that he got very little or no loving; or he had to pay a great price for what he got as a child—he had to change himself in many ways that were hurtful to him to get what he wanted. As a result, his growth processes were stunted in infancy or in his very early years. He does not have any real connecting processes because he does not see himself as a whole, adult, separate person. He sees the other person as a reflection or extension of himself. By loving the other person, he is in reality giving to and loving himself. This works fine unless the other person talks back, differs, criticizes or in some other way declares his separateness. Then the "giver" feels he has failed, is no good, or that the other person is an ingrate. He uses the other person, not as someone with whom he can express his deep feelings, but as someone who can validate constantly that he is all right. This individual is limited in his creative, producing, and building processes as so much energy is tied up in proving himself, or lashing out at others for not giving him what he deserves. His assertion processes are infantile. He asserts himself out of what he thinks will protect him or buy him what he wants rather than out of what he really feels. His real feelings are almost unknown to him because he has been so busy all his life figuring out what others want, how to please them and how to protect himself against them. As a result, he has never felt secure enough to really learn about and understand himself.

D. The "Super-Male" and "Super-Female." These are the individuals who are superficially male or female because each has based maleness and femaleness on some image he or she or someone else has made up, and they utilize a tremendous amount of energy in maintaining that image and repressing any impulses which do not fit it. These are people who experienced a tremendous sense of isolation and loneliness in their growing-up experience. Their parents may have both been there, done and said all the right things, given excellent physical care and provided the "best" for the child, but they never shared their inside feelings. They may have been model parents, but they were never real people. As a result, the child never experienced real contact. He only knows and understands pseudo contact—an imitation of the real thing. Everyone appears to be close and loving and caring and interacting; but no one is feeling anything, or if he is he isn't expressing it, or it doesn't match what he is expressing. It is like watching someone laugh, talk, cry—you hear the words and sounds and see all the expression, but you don't feel a thing. Children growing up with this kind of experience are puzzled and frightened. It looks to them on the surface as though they have everything—their home looks happy—how come they feel so badly? When everyone in the family pretends things are fine when they aren't, the child has to assume that they are crazy, he is crazy, or that is just the way it is—things are not as they seem to be. He then proceeds to join 'em rather than fight 'em and begins to build his own imitation of life with the raw material of movies, novels, phantasies, and daydreams. These people function like machines—they marry, make love, work, produce mechanistically as though the function is all there is to the human organism. They appear to have developed all the growth processes, but appearance is sham, because all their processes are based on performance and imitation; none occur as the direct expression of the individual's insides. They make connections on a functional level—to make the "right" marriage, to be a good mother or father or provider, to be helpful. Building, creating, producing, and asserting develop out of functional needs and performance without feeling. You do these things because they are the right thing to do, because that is what everyone else does to be happy; but mostly because if you didn't imitate you would not know what else to do. This individual has grown up around people who never shared real feeling. He doesn't know how to get in touch with what he really feels, doesn't even know what that means. He only knows how to function on the basis of what is right, acceptable, normal, and supposed to produce a happy ending. It does not occur to him to look to his insides for direction in his life because he has never heard of such a thing. His rhythm process is interfered with totally. These people either operate like automatons or they are sloths. They see other people as other machines or objects and relate to them as such. Mike Nichols's film *Carnal Knowledge* was a beautifully vivid portrayal of people like this. None of then has any internal understanding of what a connection with another adult really is. It is out of the realm of their experience. They often come into therapy because the way they operate continues to encourage their isolation and pain, but they know no other way. It is necessary to break through the façades they have developed to protect themselves and take care of themselves, and get to the frightened, deprived child underneath to teach that child how to become a man or a woman.

Part Two:

The Intimate
Connection

Chapter Eight:

Developing the Ability to Connect

Marriage, just like maleness and femaleness in our culture, has been based on externals. People marry because it is the expected thing to do, and because our society is based on male-female combinations. Individuals without a partner in tow feel, and literally are, left out in many instances. We are so family oriented that the individual is almost a freak. People often marry just in order not to be alone—"we two against the world."

Many women marry as though that is their only aim in life, apparently expecting that every woman is guaranteed maximum fulfillment by managing a home and having children. Women have helped maintain their second-place-citizen category by perpetrating and sustaining this myth. I suspect that child rearing is a creative process for only a relatively small percentage of men and women. Many couples have children and then do the best job they can because they are stuck with them. Some don't mind, many enjoy their children occasionally; but very few parents experience child rearing as a fulfilling, creative expression of themselves. There is no reason why they should, any more than everyone ought to enjoy and feel creative doing bookkeeping or writing or playing music. I cannot understand why we live with the assumption that everyone should find satisfaction in children just because we are biologically capable of having them.

Beautiful

Historically, of course, having as many children as possible was necessary for the survival of the race. The high infant-mortality rate, the shorter life-span, and the absence of automation meant that a high birthrate was needed to keep things going. Children began to carry their own weight very early on ranches and farms. In our current society, children are a financial and emotional burden on parents often for up to twenty-five years; and they may give little, if anything, back during that time. This is not a criticism, necessarily, of either parents or children. It is more a statement about our cultural shift. Although having children is no longer a survival necessity, we seem to continue birthing automatically. This is, probably, often because historical precedence and cultural expectations determine that is what you usually do when you get married. It would be a tremendous gift to children if only those adults who experience creative satisfaction in nurturing the growth of the young were to have children. Even if both parents do experience such satisfaction with children, however, it is unlikely that a woman's total creative capacity would be absorbed in this process alone. Yet, because many women see the role of parent as the focus of their identity rather than just as one expression of identity, they do not explore and define who they are in broader and more enriching terms. I do not believe that the maternal role in child rearing is sex differentiated. If we were not culturally educated to the contrary, some fathers in our society would achieve greater satisfaction in the home rearing the children than in any other job outside of the house. The child does not automatically associate the role of child rearer with femaleness—he or she is taught that association.

Most people marry without knowing who they really are as individuals and, least of all, who the potential marriage partner is. Thus, the relationship often begins in phantasy. The "chemistry" that we hear about so much as happening instantaneously on meeting is based, I believe, on one or both of two phenomena. First, the vibrations or aura that emanates from another individual may remind me of myself or someone who I have loved. By vibrations, I mean the subliminal messages. For example, have you ever walked into a room to join a group of other people and suddenly felt depressed? You felt fine before you came into the room and no one has yet said or done anyting—you simply picked up waves of feeling. Your antennae may not always be accurate, or you may not understand what you are receiving, but people do communicate on a level beyond words or action. This is particularly evident in the behavior of small infants. When held by different people, they will perceive tension, relaxation, or fear within the individual and respond accordingly. Adults frequently do not understand because as we get older we do not trust that level of communication and so tend to deny it exists or ignore it. However, we do respond on that level all the time, but are not aware of it or call it something else—like love at first sight. I may be perceiving something very real from the other person. The phantasy is the interpretation and conclusion I put on that perception. For example, you may seem a little fearful to me when I first meet you. I interpret that as meaning you are insecure and unsure of yourself. I immediately feel better because if you are insecure then I am in control, and I feel more comfortable when I am in control. I mistake that feeling of comfort for "kinship" or "chemistry." All of this is going on outside my awareness.

What is in my awareness is my conclusion that we are sympatico. With time and exploration, that conclusion may be found to be totally erroneous. However, we may not take the time, expecially if you complement my phantasy with your own. You may pick up my bravado and interpret that as strength and assurance, which makes you comfortable, because then you have someone to lean on who will take responsibility for you so that you won't have to make decisions you don't want to make. We may then both assume we have found what we have been looking for all our lives and we don't even try to explore any deeper. We just continue to operate as though our original assumptions and conclusions were universally true. Then our marriage is based on the rigid structure that I am the strong, assured male who makes decisions easily and you are the soft, passive female who needs to be taken care of.

The problem with that arrangement is that there is no room for growth. I can never show my uncertainty, pain, or my own need to be taken care of. You can never show your power, assertiveness, or strength, even when you feel like it. Therefore, I begin to feel overburdened and unappreciated and you feel dominated, unimportant, and repressed. We both are resentful and blame the other: "Why doesn't he give me room to be myself?" "Why doesn't she appreciate what I sacrifice for her?" Therefore, the overall underlying phantasy in the relationship is that "you owe me a good marriage and happiness—after all, you said you loved me!" Neither takes full responsibility for himself or herself. Obviously, the marriage is the culmination of the lifelong search for the "good parent"—the ultimate phantasy. It is evident, then, that relationships can be built phantasy on top of phantasy. Then if growth does occur, either through some life experience, therapy, or some other route, the phantasies begin to disintegrate and there may not be anything real in the relationship.

The other chemistry phenomenon which occurs is that the other person's looks or personality are such that it is possible for us to superimpose our lifelong dream prince or princess upon him or her. This is possible when the other person is closed off emotionally—does not reveal his feelings, even subliminally, but presents a façade. The façade may be a very pleasing one—considerate, flattering, thoughtful. However, I can't feel the other person's feelings. Since I can't, I'll have him feel what I want him to feel—love, warmth, and a desire to give to me. On the other hand, he looks at me and sees a cool, calm, collected exterior. I don't reveal my feelings either. So, he superimposes his dream on me—the "mystery" woman, cool on the outside, but deep smoldering embers on the inside only looking for the best man to crack the ice and get the goodies. The phantasy base of our relationship is that I need a fairy godfather who will pour out goodies even though I don't lift a finger; and, he needs a challenge—an immovable object which he can conquer with his irresistible force. This marriage is a protection for both of us in that neither makes a demand for the other to express his or her real feelings. In fact, the nature of our phantasy base enforces that we don't express our true feelings. As long as we both play our parts, we are safe. However, neither of us is getting any real contact. We are living with a façade in the marriage as well as individually. Our whole world is phantasy. We are afraid of anything real because we don't know how to handle it. If I begin to try to respond to you and give to you, you pull away because the challenge is no longer there. It looks as though you want me to give back to you. All our friends can't understand why you stay with me. However, you don't really want a response. You want the challenge. That makes you feel alive and it protects you from real contact. The search for the Holy Grail (me—the unattainable object) prevents you from having to deal with the problems back home (you and your dissatisfaction, pain, or anxiety). If, on the other hand, you begin to get a little tired of the challenge because you are not getting much out of it, and you stop giving to me, then I may withdraw totally from you or become bitchy and complaining. Both of these moves are distancing maneuvers although the bitchiness may look as if I am trying to make contact. The way I'm doing it is distancing, although the words are saying I want to be close to you. It is as though I am asking you for contact by beating you over the head—a contradictory message, to say the least. This is a typical pattern in this marriage. The phantasy is that we want to be close and loving. The reality is we avoid this religiously. The result is we may both get very depressed or we will look elsewhere and start the phantasy anew with someone else.

Of course it is possible that on first sight or very early in the relationship, a liking or comfortableness or excitement may develop based on very real and positive qualities. However, it is impossible to make an accurate interpretation or conclusion about such perceptions without time and experience with the other person. You may perceive a kind of softness emanating from another person. That may signal a deep warmth and tenderness or it may really cover a fearful, withdrawn state of being. Someone may project an attitude of directness, openness, and assurance. That may really mean he or she is in charge of self; or, it may mean that person likes to control others or the situation and is fine as long as he or she is not challenged. When challenged, that person feels threatened and may become devious or withdrawn. The façade of openness and directness then is revealed as a paper shell. Nothing but time and experience can reveal where another person is in terms of the internal areas of expression I have described in my earlier chapter. In addition, no matter how realistic we become or how much we know about ourselves, each of us operates with some phantasy in our romantic choices. It takes time to sort out what is real and what is unreal in the area of what we really like and want. That time needs to be filled with revelation and exploration. If I keep expressing my real feelings to you—my demands for what I want, my limitations about what I can and cannot give, my warmth, anger, sadness, hurt—straight from my insides, you either have to begin to come out equally straight with your feelings or walk away from me. It is impossible to manipulate or play games indefinitely with someone who is committed to being clear about honestly expressing who he or she is. For example:

He *(at cocktail party)*: Hello. What's your name?
She *(tells him. They carry on a get-acquainted conversation. She notices that all the while they are talking he keeps looking around the room.)*: I'm interested in continuing this conversation, but it bothers me that you keep looking around. Are you missing someone?
He *(laughs uneasily, looks embarrassed)*: Oh no, sorry. *(Makes one or two more comments, and then excuses himself.)*

She gave him a very clear message that she doesn't let herself be depreciated. He was putting her in a bind in that his words and behavior didn't match. His words were directed at her but his behavior was directed elsewhere. She could continue the conversation and feel depreciated by his wandering eye; or, she could just let the conversation die and walk away; or she could confront him. She chose to do the last in order to make herself feel better.

Another example:

She: Where would you like to go?
He: How about a movie?
She: I thought maybe we could drop in over at the Jones's!

He: I can't stand them. If you want to go it's o.k. with me, but I'll do something else.

She *(grudgingly)*: Well, then, let's go to a movie. *(sighs heavily)*

He: How about . . . *(he names a title)*?

She: I've seen that.

He: *(Names several others he would like.)*

She: None of those really sounds too good.

He: I'll tell you—since you don't seem to like my suggestions, you decide on a movie or something else you might like to do and let me know. I'm going to read the paper while you're thinking.

His message to her is that he will not be trapped into a "guilt trip" where he is knocking himself out trying to find something else that will please her because he feels guilty about setting a limit regarding the Jones's. He does not feel he needs to be all things to all people and intends to respect his limitations without apology.

Another example:

She: I'm sorry I'm not a better wife to you.

He *(feeling irritated)*: You know, I'm irritated the minute you say that and I don't know why. What are you really trying to say to me?

She *(tearful)*: You don't seem to really appreciate me and how much I count on you.

He: I'm waiting . . .

She: Why didn't you take the car in like you promised— you know how much I was counting on it!

He: I'm an unfeeling, disinterested lout. Would you like me to cut off one of my fingers?—or better still, my . . .

She *(interrupting)*: Now you're being ridiculous . . .

He: I'm sorry about the car—I forgot. I don't mind your being annoyed about that, but I won't be made to feel like the executioner at a hanging— I have not ruined your whole life!

He is picking up two messages from her—the overt one as the hurt, injured party and the covert message coming from her via the needle. He is making it clear he will respond to her direct anger, but not the needle.

Some people marry as a way of running away from themselves. For example, I may marry you because you may seem to need rescuing in some way. Perhaps you had a miserable childhood and I want to make that up to you; or, maybe your first marriage was to a cad or a bitch. Maybe you are helpless like a little boy or a little girl and I want to take care of you. If I marry you and concentrate on making everything all right for you, then I don't have to look at me. If I had to focus on me, I might be aware of a kind of gnawing anxiety or depression that I don't understand. I want to run away from those feelings because I cannot explain them and I am afraid those feelings may be an indication of something I don't want to look at (my relationships or my job or some very important area of my life isn't working for me); and, it might mean making some changes I don't want to face. If I had to look at me, perhaps I'd find I'm not really satisfied with where I am or what I'm doing; if I let myself see that, then I would have to do something about it, and I'm afraid to take risks and experiment in my life. I grew up in a family where experimenting and risk-taking were discouraged as foolish, not sensible, or potentially destructive. Maybe I'd rather stay in my dull job and get my kicks and satisfaction out of taking care of my alcoholic wife who certainly provides me with plenty of excitement—jail, hysteria, and other periodic uproars—and who makes me feel useful so I don't have to consider that I may be wasting my life and my potential.

An individual may marry someone in order to solve his own problems—"I'm miserable, nothing works out right for me, I never get the breaks. Maybe, if I marry you, things will get better for me. After all, it's a new beginning." Maybe the other person is miserable too, but "two miserable people are better than one miserable person alone." Perhaps, in some instances, that is so. However, most of the time that sort of marriage is an escape for each individual involved, from dealing with his and her own individual problems. Instead of solving anything, the marriage tends to multiply the problems since each person's depressions and anxiety reenforces and feeds that of the other. In addition, resentment builds in both because the partner is not making things better as he or she was supposed to do. Each is a constant disappointment to the other for not having brought happiness into the union; and, the marriage also keeps each person from really working on the root of his own unhappiness because he can always blame the other. Marriages like this can go on for years—look and be perfectly miserable. However, they continue because apparently it would be too terrifying to the individuals involved to have to consider change. Many people would rather stay with familiar misery than risk the unfamiliar and unknown territory of change and growth.

There are people who marry because one or both really do have a tremendous desire for children, and perhaps both are talented parents who would get tremendous satisfaction from being a part of a child's growth process. However, if the desire for progeny is the basis of the marital relationship, then the children bear a tremendous burden to make it all worthwhile. They cannot help but get the message that the parent is living for them instead of for himself. For children to feel separate as people and therefore free to grow in their own ways, they have to be the by-product of the relationship, not the be-all and end-all.

There is a kind of marriage in which "I am one half of a pair of scissors and you are the other half—I need you in order to complete me and make me whole." For example, I want to be normal. My program determines that normality means being married and having children. You have the same program. Therefore, we need each other to make us feel normal. Another example: "I don't make friends easily, feel awkward and never know what to say. You are gregarious and seem to meet people easily. I need you to provide company for me; then I don't need to learn how to do that for myself. That's O.K. with you because you like to be the center of attention and don't want competition." Or, "people are always taking advantage of me. I get angry about it but I don't let anyone know because then they wouldn't like me or wouldn't think I was generous and nice. You, on the other hand, seem to be able to tell people off very easily. I need you to keep people from taking advantage of me, so you can be the ogre and I can keep my image. You may seem to be expressive, in some instances, but you also have a lot of anger which you don't express directly, but store it up and contain it; so, it's a relief to you to have an underdog for whom you can legitimately fight, thus releasing your anger in a Good Cause. If you expressed it just for yourself with no justifiable reason, you might be considered selfish and you were taught not to be selfish or no one would love you."

In all of these liaisons, the phantasy base is any one or a combination of these: I need you to make me whole or complete me in some way; I need you for protection against the world; I need you to keep me from having to face parts of myself I don't want to see; or, I need you to get what I can't get on my own. The creative connection process based on sharing, mutual enhancement, and fulfillment is blocked or totally unknown in these relationships because the focus of all energy in the relationship goes toward using the relationship to protect the survival of the individuals involved— they are convinced they cannot survive alone—or to validate and prove their worth. In order to connect in an enhancing way, the individual must be comfortable in his autonomy and aloneness. Real and deep connections are possible only out of separateness and autonomy.

Chapter Nine:

Separateness and Autonomy

I believe that the individual is born with all the necessary parts emotionally as well as physically and mentally. If the newborn is physically or mentally damaged or incomplete, there may be damage or incompleteness to the emotional apparatus as well—I don't know. My exploration has been only with individuals who have been physically and mentally normal without brain damage, crippling, or missing physical parts; so I will deal here only with the complete organism.

The child is not born with any emptiness or holes in his makeup that adults must fill. He is a total unique organism, complete with fully developed embryonic ego (in psychological terms), a sense of who he is and what he needs (in other terms). He has two primary requirements of his parents: he needs nurturing in the form of physical care and body contact—the more lavish the better; and he needs space.

You cannot over-nurture an infant. Infants do not manipulate. Granted, they will try to get more than they need for
immediate growth, but that is the organism's natural striving
for survival and pleasure, not manipulation. If the child gets
more than he or she immediately needs, he will not waste it.
It will be stored in his emotional bank of riches which he can
fall back on later if he needs it. Therefore, response to an
infant's need for being held, for affection and time with the
parent, should be based on what the parents can give without
hurting themselves and not on what an infant should have
because he can't have too much. However, it is important to
his well-being that parents take good care of themselves as
well as of him. It is the same thing. Children, especially infant
children, are masters at "inside communication." We are born
knowing how to feel and this is our primary means of
communication long before we learn how to talk. I believe
there is even communication between mother and child in
the womb and hope that, someday, we can explore this
phenomenon in depth. This "inside communication" is the
primary reason why body contact with the parent is absolutely essential for a child's healthy growth. There cannot be too
much unless it becomes intrusive to him, and he will quickly
let you know about that. The child takes pleasure in the
contact and warmth, but more important, he can feel the
parent's inside feelings. If you don't believe that, try holding
your infant child at different times when you are in varying
emotional states and watch the difference in his response.

The child's ability to feel the parent's feelings, particularly
those directed at him, give him a sense of belonging, of being
loved and cared for, which in turn offers him stability and
security. A child can be cared for beautifully in terms of
having all his physical needs met and even getting considerable body contact; but, if the parenting figure has no deep
feelings for the child or does not allow himself to feel those
deep feelings, the child's emotional growth will be greatly

disrupted or even impaired. Ideally, then, it is important that
the parent take care of his or her own needs for rest,
enjoyment, space away from the child, nurturing between
spouses, and other creative satisfactions. If the parents do not
take good care of themselves, they will automatically be
limited in what they can communicate on this level. When a
human being is exhausted or emotionally drained, this area of
deep emotional outpouring is the first to suffer. There is a
deadening effect, like a well run dry. With rest and care, the
well will quickly fill up again. Without this, the well will
always operate at a barely adequate level. The child is then
automatically emotionally undernourished. I understand that
parents cannot always take care of themselves when a child's
needs are pressing or when the external situation puts un-
usual pressures on the family. What I am saying is that there
are no rules for being a good parent. It is a matter of establishing, as much as possible, a balance between meeting the
child's needs and meeting your own because they are really
one and the same. By that, I mean there is a flow between
parent and child, based on that balance, that is the most
nourishing and vital process to the child's growth.

The second primary requirement the infant has is for
space. It is vital that he not be intruded upon. Intrusion has
many forms. Parents can intrude by forcing the child to eat
and sleep on a schedule rather than according to his natural
rhythm which is different for every child. They can intrude
by picking the child up or giving him affection when he
doesn't want it. Children are quite different in this respect.
Some want to be cuddled often and seem to melt into your
arms. Others will get stiff in your arms, making it clear they
want to be put down. Children have an infinite variety of
needs unique to each and will make those needs quite clear if
the parent can pay attention without putting value judgments
on the child's needs—i.e., "He doesn't love me, he never
wants me to hold him."

Another form of intrusion has to do with the emotional state of the person caring for the child. A child needs parents who have developed processes for handling their tensions, differences, and low emotional states satisfactorily, so that he does not receive constant perceptual stimuli of pain from the people taking care of him. Such constant stimulus produces anxiety in the child and takes him away from focusing on his own expanding awareness and growth. I don't mean to imply that the parent has to be in optimum emotional shape every time he or she goes near the child; but, a mother who harbors unresolved resentment against her husband over a long period of time, communicates her dissatisfaction and tension to the child simply by being close to him. He may respond by being restless, sick, irritable, or withdrawn. Infants can handle all kinds of ups and downs with extreme emotional upheaval in a family without any long-lasting ill effects as long as the parents are facing their problems and their feelings and dealing directly with themselves and each other about them. During times of extreme stress in a family, like a severe illness or job change or move, the infant will normally react with a slower growth flow or even with a regression. For example, he may go back to crawling when he has just started walking. However, he will quickly resume when the crisis is passed and often even have a growth spurt then. What is really intrusive to his growth is repressed, unresolved feeling in his parents. They may think they are living with their repressed feelings adequately, but such repression produces in them a kind of low-level tension to which the child is acutely attuned. This kind of ongoing, low-level tension message produces anxiety in the child because it interferes with his contact with the parent. The dissatisfaction with which the mother is living is draining her when it continues over a long period of time, and it interferes with the love, tenderness and warmth she feels for the child. So, the child is getting less warmth than he would otherwise, and what he is getting is not communicated to him clearly. He is constantly perceiving two messages at the same time—warmth and tension. As a result, he has to split his energy to deal with his own growth needs and also with the tension he is receiving. He has to develop ways to protect himself against the tension messages he is receiving. Since all his energy is not directed toward his growth, his growth process will be impaired in varying degrees depending on how much tension the parent is carrying and how much native energy the child has. I think there are innate differences in the natural energy capacity of each child. If the child has a high energy capacity, he may be able to handle a fairly high degree of tension without severe impairment to his growth. However, there would still be impaired growth potential because all of his energy would not be available for growth.

As the child becomes older and is more in charge of himself, the intrusion factor becomes even more important. I believe that if it were not for the intrusion by the parents, most children would be obviously unique and very unlike either parent. I think that what is actually inherited is miniscule. It would be the exception rather than the rule that any child would resemble his parents in personality. Intrusion takes many forms—some quite subtle. For example, we seldom take into consideration what the difference in physical size between adults and children means to the child. You often see an adult walking along with a very small child, holding his hand, and the adult wonders why the child gets obstreperous and cranky after a few minutes of this. Try holding your hand straight up in the air for longer than thirty seconds and see how uncomfortable that is. As adults, we often carry on a conversation with a small child who is looking up at us while we are standing. Try holding your head that far back and looking up for any length of time. It would be difficult to concentrate on what someone else was saying while holding yourself in that position.

Adults often take physical liberties with children—grabbing a child's hand without warning or permission, picking him up and holding him or placing him somewhere else without consulting him or even against his will when there is no particular reason for the action. It isn't that we are unfeeling or insensitive as adults. It is simply that most of us operate as though children are not people. They do not have the judgment, experience and knowledge that adults have and therefore must be taken care of while these attributes develop and are taught. However, they have everything else we have including a sense of boundaries about their persons. They do not like to be violated in this respect any more than you would like some other adult whooshing you off your feet and putting you somewhere you may or may not want to go.

Adults will often speak for a child as though the child does not know what he thinks or feels. At times I have asked a two- or three-year-old child a question and the parent will immediately answer for him—"He doesn't know what you mean," "He doesn't understand," He doesn't know what he feels yet." I used to make the same kind of assumptions until I started working with families in therapy. I always included even very young children in the sessions and tried talking to them seriously. Not only do they know what they think and feel, but they can often tell you the problem in the family faster and more clearly than anyone else. I was working with a family once with two children, four and six. I asked the four-year-old boy what he did when Mom and Dad disagreed. He said, "I have a temper tantrum." I asked him why he did that and he replied, "I have to save them," referring to his parents. Needless to say, that broke the ice in the session. The parents realized that the fact they were contemplating divorce was no secret to the children even though they didn't talk about it openly, and they were then able to begin to discuss some of their difficult problems openly in the session. I have learned great respect for very small children. They are

closer to their feelings than most of us and have not yet
learned how to use words to cover or hide what they feel.

Adults often interrupt children without apology or explanation. I realize children have to be taught how to make space for others in conversation; and, perhaps there are times when they are welcome to join in conversation and other times when conversation is restricted to adult participation, whatever the family rules. However, these kinds of limits can always be set with regard for the child's feelings, just as you would with another adult. The human organism, for maximum growth, needs to be treated with dignity, whatever the age. This involves respect for his physical boundaries—asking permission to pick him up, hold him or kiss him if he isn't giving clear messages that it is all right; and explaining what you are doing and why, when it isn't possible to include him in a decision that involves his boundaries (he needs physical care or intervention beyond his ability to totally understand or cooperate). Such explanation can be given even to a preschool child. He may not understand the words but he gets a considerate message from the tone and manner of the parent. Treating the child with dignity also involves taking his feelings into consideration in the same manner that you, hopefully, would consider another adult. Consider his feelings in making decisions that involve him. When you have to make a decision about him that is opposite to what he feels, give him room to express his disappointment or resentment. The message then to him is—he has a right to his feelings. Any attempt to control how another person feels is an intrusion which builds resentment and distance between any two people, not just parents and children. Parents can often successfully govern a child's behavior, but they can in no way control or govern how he feels. In fact, it is often much easier to get a child to cooperate with the family rules about behavior if there is plenty of room, without infringement on the parents' rights or persons, for the child to express his feelings. Again, there needs to be a balanced flow between parents and children for expressing feeling both ways, without intrusion, so that each person has room to be himself without a loss to all the others. Parents need to be very clear with children what their own boundaries are in this respect. For example, mother might say, "If you're angry with me you can tell me that you hate me, but don't hit me." Father might say, "If you're angry, I'll get on my knees and we can have a boxing match as long as you don't hit me in the face, but don't tell me you hate me—." Each parent lets the child know what his limits are in his ability to hear and respond to the child. The limits are presented, not as what is right or wrong or good or bad, but what the parent likes or does not like, what he can hear or what turns him off. Thus, the family unit becomes the training ground for the development of communication based on clear expression of self plus respect for the boundaries and dignity of others.

Adults often intrude on children by superimposing their own distorted assumptions about what is male and female. We bombard children with messages in this area from the moment of birth. We do it verbally by labeling certain activities, physical characteristics and mannerisms as male or female and encouraging their development on that basis. We do it nonverbally by buying "masculine" toys for boy and "feminine" toys for girls and pushing the toys on that basis. We do it by facial expression—looking pained or nervous when he wants to play with a doll or she wants to explore a tool chest. Most children are brainwashed by the family and community standards of maleness and femaleness by the time they are five or six.

We intrude on children by assuming that we really can control them, and we try to do this with judgments like good or bad, right or wrong. The truth is no one can really control anyone else without that person's cooperation. Children often cooperate because they need us, love us and aren't all that sure of themselves. However, they begin making choices for themselves very early. By the time a child is six years old, he is away from home five to seven hours a day—at school or outside playing. During that time, he is constantly making choices for himself—how he will respond to the teacher, how he will respond to the other children, whom he wants for friends, what he wants to do, what is scary to him and what is pleasant, what risks he can take and what he should avoid or isn't yet ready for. As adults, we need to respect this reality and understand that children really are in charge of themselves, under our jurisdiction; and, with growth, they will be taking more and more responsibility for themselves with less need for structure from us. Children need direction, guidance and structure in the form of discipline via choices. This takes discipline and direction off the framework of whether or not you love me, whether or not you want to hurt me, whether or not you are good, bad, right, wrong. All of these messages are intrusive. These messages confuse and disrupt the child's insides so that he is no longer clear about who he is and what he wants. He gets what he wants confused with what he should want and he is immobilized. If the message from the parent is strictly a matter of choice—"You do what I ask or you'll pay a tangible price"—that may be annoying, but it leaves the child intact. I don't mean that parents should not communicate their values and moral standards to their children. Of course that communication is important. But, such standards need to be presented by parents as their own without the attempt to enforce them on the child. That is really impossible to do and the attempt to do so simply drives a wedge between parent and child. The parent needs to recognize that the child will form his own standards and the most helpful thing the parent can do is to make clear his own values but keep them out of the discipline area.

The child also needs the quality of "solidity" from his

parents. By this, I mean that whenever he asserts himself, he always gets a clear message from the parent about how the parent feels in response to what the child says or does. In additon, he gets equally clear messages from parents about how they are feeling inside about themselves so he does not have to guess or be afraid. The child is still communicating on the "inside" level and, different than most adults, he still relies on that level of communication more than any other. So, if the parent is saying everything is all right, and the child is perceiving feelings of tension or sadness, he is confused and frightened. The child concludes that the parent is saying to him that certain feelings are too dangerous to express and that message gets in the way of the child commenting on what he perceives from the parents or expressing those kinds of feelings when he is upset. If that double-message process is common in the family—outward serenity coupled with inward tension—then the child begins to feel he cannot trust the parents, that they are not reliable for him. Those parental responses and assertions that are important to a child do not have to do with fairness, goodness, rightness, or objectivity. They have to do with clear, congruent messages about what the parent is feeling. He likes something, he doesn't like it. He is angry, he is sad. He is feeling low; he had a bad day "so everybody go away." He cries when he feels like it; he mopes when he feels like it; he may even have a temper tantrum when he feels that way inside. The child gets the message that feelings are valuable and not dangerous because the parent says and does what he really feels inside, not what he thinks is right or perfect. That gives the child permission and encouragement to own and express his own feelings.

The parent's clear expression of himself is a distinct relief to the child even if he doesn't like or agree with what the parent is saying or doing. If the parent says "Knock it off, you bug me!" rather than "You are not being nice" or "You are wrong and inconsiderate to make so much noise" the child may be annoyed at having to stop what he is doing, but he does not feel less as a person. The message the parent is sending is a statement about himself—what he wants or doesn't want—not a judgment about the child. The child needs to be responded to, given to, disciplined, talked to, and related to in ways that may sometimes take away privileges or rights, but do not infringe on his dignity as a person or violate his boundaries. The infringement message is "If you loved me," or "If you were good, you would be like I want you to be." He can tolerate changing his behavior to suit you if you, as the parent, recognize that he has the right to feel differently than you do without a loss to his self-esteem.

If parents provide this kind of structure, then the child is free to experiment. He can act on his feelings and feel free to express himself, knowing that he will get "sat on" at times but never belittled, cut down, or lessened. Thus the home becomes his primary experimental arena to test himself, find out what really fits him and what doesn't. He can act out his feelings rather than repress them or distort them to please others. Through the action and the subsequent honest responses of his parents, he can find out which ways of behaving he wants to keep and which he wants to change or discard. In this way, he defines himself internally, and develops a solid sense of himself as a whole person. He learns that he can get what he wants by being who he is. He may have to learn to modify or change the ways he uses to express himself so that they connect better with others as well as express his insides, but he does not have to change who he is. He has received the message from his family that the person he is is respected and that his growth has to do with learning to express and develop that person most effectively. That is a powerful message. The child grows into an adult who is clear and secure in the knowledge that he is most effective by being himself. He can survive and get what he needs without sham, pretense, manipulation, or distortion. That knowledge is the basis of the individual's sense of himself as a whole, autonomous person.

When the parents do not provide this kind of solid response to the child, the child stops the exploration of his insides via the route of asserting himself in the family. He does not trust the mixed messages he is getting. When it seems to him that his parents are not saying and doing what they really feel, he may respond in one or more of several ways. He may withdraw and be afraid to assert at all. He may stop focusing on what he feels and start trying to learn to read his parents' minds—he will try to figure out what they are feeling by using subtle nuances and signs in their expression or behavior about which he then makes assumptions and conclusions. For example, his father may say that everything is all right, but his face looks a little strained around the mouth. The child assumes his father is angry and then he goes about searching through the day's events to try to figure out what his father is angry about so that he, the child, can make everything all right again. Since the clues he is using are so subtle, his interpretations may not always be accurate. Therefore, he is in a continuing state of anxiety because he never knows for sure where he stands with the parent. He is always afraid he will do or say the wrong thing and no one will tell him; or, if they do tell him, they will assume that he intended to be bad or hurtful and erred on purpose out of disrespect for them or a desire to hurt them. The reality is he might disobey on purpose, but it would not be directed at them; it would be an attempt to follow his own interest and get by with it.

Such a response or lack of response from parents lays the base for the child to become an expert manipulator. He learns the best way to get what he wants without looking as if he is getting what he wants so that he won't be labeled selfish, hurtful, wrong, or bad. He learns to keep his feelings to himself and get what he wants by shifting the responsibility for his feelings and behavior to someone else—i.e., "I took the money from your purse (when caught in the act) because you were mean to me"; "I didn't tell the truth because I was afraid you would hit me (to a parent who has never hit him)"; "I did that because I thought you wanted me to"; "I was only trying to help, protect, give to you"; "I wasn't honest because I didn't want to hurt you"; and on and on.

Another way a child might adjust is to adopt his parents' structure of what is good and right, not because he really agrees with them and feels the way they do, but because it gets them off his back and wins their approval. He will adapt his functioning to fit this structure and repress all feelings that do not seem to fit into this framework. Whichever of these ways he goes, he shifts from growing by experimenting with expressing who he is inside of himself to adopting a structure which doesn't necessarily fit him but which enables him to survive (be acceptable and not isolated) and grow. His survival then becomes dependent on his ability to manipulate and please others, and to keep them from finding out who he really is.

As an example, let's look at a family in which the parents are experiencing a great deal of pain—either they are not getting what they need, or they are under great external pressure because of responsibilities. They are not opening up with their pain, but are pretending everything is fine; or they are having uproarious fights that don't seem to go anywhere. Therefore, the child may respond to the mixed message and his parents' pain with rebellion in a delinquent pattern as an expression of his own pain, inner confusion and lack of self-esteem. They have unknowingly put him in a bind. He feels their pain and cannot comment on it because they have made it clear by their avoidance that it is in some way dangerous to do so. His behavior looks as though he is saying "I don't care about anybody in this family!" More accurately, he is expressing his own real pain and confusion as well as drawing the focus in the family away from the pain of his parents he becomes a scapegoat to protect the parents from having to deal with themselves. He assumes they are saying, by their avoidance of their pain, that they cannot deal with it and need to be rescued. As long as everyone focuses on the child, they don't have time or energy to look at their own problems. On some deep level, the child feels he is saving his family and therefore himself, since he needs them. The problem is that no one in the family is getting very much and everyone's growth is severly inhibited by this way of handling their problems.

When adults who have grown up in any of these kinds of frameworks come into therapy, they often express a feeling of emptiness inside and project the message that the therapist must fill them up and take care of them. They are not really empty or missing any parts. It is just that their life experience has not provided them with the family structure in which they could learn to define who they are from the inside. Thus, their insides are unknown territory. It is as though "I know all about how to manipulate and please you—I've spent my life learning that—but I don't know anything at all about me. My focus has always been to define myself around what someone else wants or needs." Once the individual understands this, he can begin to use the therapist as someone solid against whom he can test out his innermost feelings. It isn't necessary that the therapist be an ideal or model person—I don't know what that is, anyway—it is necessary that he or she be in charge of self and able to manifest who he is as a total person clearly and congruently. I see therapy as a process in which the therapist and the client let each other experience who they are as people and through which both grow. The client, with the help of the therapist's solid responses to him and the therapist's expert knowledge about growth processes, learns how to focus in on himself and explore his real self. The therapist learns more about himself in relation to this particular person and more about human uniqueness in general. When my clients begin to give me honest responses about how they see me and feel towards me, I am always learning something new about myself; and it is an exciting experience for me to have the opportunity to view an emerging individual. Much of this book has come out of such experience.

It is amazing to me how much of our "sameness" is due to family and cultural pressures. As the individual surmounts these pressures to emerge on his own, I am constantly awed by the uniqueness of each individual. What a vast ocean of untapped resource is humanity. Everything in nature is part of a constant flow—parts die while other parts are growing, and parts grow even when the whole organism is dying. The natural state of the human organism is one of constant ebb and flow of change. Yet, most of our cultural and educational and even family experience is directed toward putting us into stable, predictable, unchanging states of being. We grow up preferring the familiar and predictable, which is really against our nature. I am awed by what our capabilities might be if we were taught from the beginning of life to respect, appreciate, and listen to the natural, rhythmic flow of our own individual growth processes; and to see change, not as something to fear or avoid at all costs, but as life itself.

Chapter Ten:

The Absence of "Fit" in Male-Female Connections

It is possible for individuals to be separate and autonomous, to care about each other, to connect in important areas (like the ability to mutually feel and share those deep feelings, similar value structure, similar life goals, etc.), and still not fit in an intimate relationship for any length of time. There are several reasons for this. One very important reason is that many individuals are discrepant with each other in their unique individual rhythms. As I discussed in an earlier chapter, rhythm determines the individual's innate way of meeting his world—the way he learns, meets new situations and people, eats, sleeps, makes love, handles frustration, adapts to his environment, and presents himself to the world. Sometimes, when a couple is in therapy and have broken down the barriers in the way of each becoming separate and clear about who he or she is, the differences in rhythm begin to be evident when they weren't before. People who are not in charge of themselves and congruent in their behavior with their insides are not totally in touch with their natural rhythms. Thus, rhythm differences get labeled as some other problem or are not even evident until people grow to the extent of experiencing themselves as whole and separate individuals. As an example, one person in the relationship needs a certain amount of organization and structure in order to move and grow comfortably. Let's say it's the husband in this instance. (Rhythm differences do not seem to me to be sex-linked.) Anyway, the husband likes to plan ahead, know where he is going next week or even a year from now in some instances, and to budget his money so that he is always fairly clear where he stands financially. He needs this kind of stability and predictability in order to flow with a minimum of tension. His natural way of handling things is steady and the flow is even. He looks at an issue, he thinks, he plans ahead and he moves all in a somewhat measured cadence. His wife, on the other hand, moves in a seemingly faster flow (moves in and out, back and forth, tries this and drops it, tries that, until she finds what fits for her). They may arrive at any goal at the same time; she doesn't necessarily get where she is going any faster than he. It is just that she flows at sixty r.p.m.'s while he goes at thirty. Now, it is possible that she may perceive him, on the basis of his rhythm, as dull, plodding, and holding her back. He can perceive her as frenetic, scatterbrained, and unreliable. Thus, each is giving the other negative messages about something basic and un-changeable about who each person is. Rhythm may be modi-fied somewhat, but the basic pattern cannot be changed. It is innate to who the individual is in the deepest part of himself.

Therefore, when someone criticizes and tries to change another person's natural rhythm, that attempt is perceived as an intrusion and as depreciation. On the receiving end, it feels something like listening to fingernails scrape on a blackboard—very painful without knowing exactly why. Now, there are important reasons why the wife, in this instance, might originally have been attracted to her husband. In her growing-up experience, her parents gave her the message that her natural rhythm was unreliable, hurtful, or unproductive. Therefore, she chose someone who could give her "stability." However, as she has grown, she has learned to appreciate and respect her natural flow and to tune in to it more. Thus, she has learned it is reliable and productive for her even though it might not be understood by her parents or husband. So what she once saw in him as stability, now becomes a source of irritation to her. On the other hand, her husband may have heard, in his growing-up experience, that his way of operating was dull and dead, so he looked to his wife for life and excitement in her different pace. However, as he grows in his ability to trust himself and his own way of operating, he has learned he can feel more alive and satisfied following his own rhythm. Therefore, what he once saw as a gift of excitement from his wife now becomes a pain in the neck.

Most of the time, people do not recognize that such differences are innate and unchangeable by an act of will. They often operate as though "If you loved me" or "If you tried harder," you could do this differently. This assumption produces frustration on the part of both people involved. They might be able to make room for the differences with a minimum of frustration and irritation if each could see that their differences have to do with who they are basically. However, sometimes they cannot make the adjustment no matter how hard they try. At times, even though the wife understands fully in the deepest parts of herself that her husband's way of operating has to do with his uniqueness and is in no way a reflection of how he feels about her and, although she may even appreciate his growth rhythm and see advantages in it that hers doesn't have, she still may not be able to tolerate it living in close proximity. She may find herself feeling intruded upon or unappreciated, resentful or deprived, even though she knows he does love her and does not intend or want to intrude on her. Her feelings are the result of the differences in their rhythms. His way of operating just does not give her what she needs and wants, and requires more adjustment on her part than she is able to make without great cost to herself. The same may be true for him. He may find he has to constantly leave his steady pattern in order to cope with her more frenetic pace; and that it is almost impossible for him to stay in touch with his own feelings and direction for himself and still relate to her. So, he feels he is constantly faced with the choice to go her way or his; it is not possible for him to be with himself and with her at the same time. When he is with her, he doesn't know what he feels or wants. He has to get off by himself to regain his balance and his sense of himself.

With another couple, her growth rhythm has a steady, forward push to it. She operates in a direct line. She sees a problem, looks at all the possible directions for solving it, figures out the pros and cons, checks how she feels about it, decides on a course of action and does it. She meets a new person, finds out all she can about that person, decides she would like to know him or her better and invites the new acquaintance to dinner. If she makes a mistake, she files that experience away for future reference, but it doesn't slow her down or alter her direct course. His rhythm, however, has an ebb and flow to it. He looks at a problem and considers it; then he may leave it and go to something else entirely. This is his way of taking space to let his insides assimilate and consider. Then he returns spontaneously to the original problem, with decision made, ready for action. So, if he makes a mistake or does something she doesn't like and she lets him know this, he may hear her but then move away into himself or into something else. If he should try to respond immediately in order to please her, the response would probably be inaccurate in terms of his real feelings. If he follows his rhythm, he will probably take his space and return later with a response that is clear. Thus, if his wife asks something of him or criticizes him and, with her direct forward rhythm, insists on an immediate response, he will feel intruded upon and pushed. She, on her part, may feel abandoned or unappreciated when she is wanting something or is upset and he takes space. When they understand this process in the light of differences in rhythm rather than evidence of noncaring or noncooperation, then it may be less painful to each of them and they may be able to develop ways of handling the differences. He may be able to tell her when he needs space and to take a firm stand to keep her from intruding on his space. This may be easier for him to do if he realizes she is intruding out of her differentness (it doesn't feel like intrusion to her, it only seems natural) and not because she wants to control him. She may be able to let him take his space, with less anxiety on her part, if she realizes he is following his natural process and not deliberately deserting her. However, it will cost each one energy to understand and appreciate that. Also, it means they will have to have interests and activities separate from each other, in which it is possible for each to flow naturally without having to make rhythm adjustments, in order to balance their relationship with each other. There are many relationships in which the rewards are so great in other areas that people can tolerate rhythm discrepancies, depending on the degree of the discrepancy. Many couples have rhythm differences because I think it takes time and experience in close proximity with the other person to become aware of these discrepancies, and many people do not explore to this extent prior to marriage.

A couple may have a similar rhythm, but the nature of the rhythm pattern is such that, occasionally, they may be out of phase. For example, let's say the male has an up-and-down pattern to his rhythm. When he is up, he is very much "there"—responsive, easy to contact, ready to get involved, available. When he is down, he appears somewhat withdrawn, rather quiet, and a little vague. His wife has a similar up-and-down pattern, although she expresses it a little differently. When up, she is vivacious, eager, energetic, and loving. When down, she is lethargic, somewhat moody, and perhaps slightly irritable.

Therefore, when they are learning something new, meeting new people, handling a problem, they are capable of many mood swings in the process of evolving a decision or a relationship or an adjustment in any situation. They may go from enthusiasm and elation to despair to boredom and back to elation. Since each has a similar rhythm, they understand this in the other and do not interpret the changes as a statement about their feelings for each other. However, the difficulty occurs when both are down or one is up and the other down for any long period of time, as for several days. At these times, they feel very distant from each other and lonely, even when the other one is physically there. Each must then have ways of handling this distance which are not hurtful to the relationship. Usually, this means going separate ways temporarily, and each taking care of self without the help or support of the other. Thus, the relationship itself develops a kind of in-and-out rhythm. They can be deeply connected and very close, yet later quite separate and even distant. As long as each understands this in terms of rhythm and knows that the periods of closeness will return if they just let themselves flow, they don't need to get frightened or distrustful of each other or of the relationship.

There are probably as many variations of rhythm as there are individuals. However, I would like to touch on a few more just to clarify the concept for you. I am really just beginning to explore what this process means in relationships. The deeper I delve into understanding individual rhythm, the more impressed I am with its importance and the need to research into the mysteries of this phenomenon. I am basing my examples on actual couples with whom I have worked in marital therapy or known personally as friends. They had all reached the point in growth where it was possible for them to perceive their individual rhythms and then use that perception as the base for promoting growth and understanding in the relationship; or for determining separation, if the rhythm difference was too painful for connection, made the connection too much work, or made the relationship not enjoyable enough for either person.

In one relationship, the male has a rhythm consisting of sharp abrupt shifts which make his behavior appear almost spastic to the observer. He can move from a state of serenity and quiet to sadness and moodiness, to playfulness, to joy, to intense activity, all in the course of one interaction; or, he can stay in each of these states for several hours or days or even longer. Regardless of the space in between, the overall pattern consists of swift, unpredictable shifts. At the peak of the outgoing part of his rhythm, he can appear flippant and self-absorbed to the point of seeming assaultive in his expression, as though he leaves no room for the other person. His wife has a soft, even rhythm with minor mood shifts that move smoothly without much ripple in the overall pattern. She looks as though she takes everything in stride, which in a sense is so, in that she is not easily "thrown." However, she goes through many ups and downs—they are just miniscule and very subtle by comparison with her husband's broad, abrupt shifts. Because of this, he may not notice her subtle nuances of change, and she may feel herself unimportant and unappreciated by him. She may also feel resentful and hurt by his abrupt assertions which are assaultive to her more even, subtle rhythm. He is puzzled and feels very misunderstood because of her reaction, since his assertion is often the result of a feeling of well-being rather than anger, and he does not experience himself as assaultive. He experiences himself as clear and direct, and her as wishy-washy and diffuse. Since they have many other things going for them in the relationship, they may be able to tolerate this difference. If they do, they then have the opportunity for growth by studying and understanding each other's rhythm and the differences between them. As he learns about her subtle nuance of behavior change, he might use that awareness of what he sees in her to begin to see and experience subtleties in his own feelings and behavior that he had not been aware of before. As she begins to see and understand some of his behavior as connected to his rhythm rather than directed as an assault at her, she can begin to look at the way he expresses himself with more objectivity on her part. She then has the opportunity to use this new knowledge to get in touch with and explore the more demanding, outgoing parts of herself she has overlooked because they were minimal in comparison to her overall pattern of operating.

The essence of a relationship is like everything in nature—a balance; in this case, the balance between sameness and differentness. The differentness in a relationship provides mutual stimulation of growth, and the sameness provides comfort. I think that the potential for depth in a relationship is greatest when the rhythm is either similar or complementary and the differentness lies in other areas. This is because rhythm differences that are intrusive or distancing require much energy to handle constructively, and always prevent the relationship from developing a really smooth flow to it no matter how well the differences are handled. As is evident in these examples, some rhythm differences require constant attention and adjustment, which automatically acts as a periodic brake on the growth of the relationship. It doesn't stop it, but it slows it down. A relationship in which the rhythms mesh is a connection on the most basic level and, therefore, can develop into a flow without stops and starts. It is like the difference between two racing cars, one of which has to make pit stops while the other can go on indefinitely.

In still another relationship, the male has what I can best describe as a rhythm within a rhythm. The transcending obvious rhythm which determines the way he handles his work, meets people, makes decisions, and otherwise directs his life, is structured in straight, strong strokes. He moves in a clear, measured, logical, firm, and direct line from problem to solution, from beginning to end, from here to there without looking back, stopping or starting. Running concurrently and in counterpoint to that rhythm is another rhythm which determines how he handles his intimate relationships, his moments of relaxation and enjoyment, and his creative processes. This rhythm is like a soft, gentle ripple, poetic in its flow, easily intruded upon and thus easily cut off or blocked. When this rhythm is prominent, his behavior is "goal-less." In a relationship, he moves from touching to talking to phantasy to imagery without direction or any focus on outcome. When outcome is important, he shifts to the other rhythm. His wife has one basic rhythm which is also strong and direct, but not measured or logical in process. She may move in and out of a situation many times before she settles on a solution or direction. She needs a lot of space for this and does not like to be pinned down. She needs to be able to hang loose so that she can shift with a minimum of stress until she finds what works for her. His basic rhythm need for direct progression makes her feel trapped and judged. He experiences her back-and-forth flow as frustrating to him and an indication of childishness and irresponsibility on her part. In addition, her broad movements and wide mood swings make it impossible for him to express himself via his other rhythm except when away from her.

Thus, exploration of the relationship with this part of himself was blocked. The rhythm differences and the misunderstandings about this caused so much pain that this couple divorced. Much later, when they could be more objective, each returned to therapy for some understanding of the reasons for the pain. He later married another woman who had a "rhythm within a rhythm" pattern similar to his own. This marriage combination worked very well and, I think, was the best possible rhythm combination for both of them. His former wife connected with a man, without marriage, whose rhythm was even looser and less structured than hers. She saw him as even more changeable than herself, which scared her a little, but was much more acceptable to her than her former husband's pattern.

One last rhythm pattern I would like to discuss is the most difficult for me to describe. The female, in this relationship, has a rhythm which has a kind of spiraling effect. She moves forward by going deeper. When she approaches a problem, she will explore in depth, not so much the factual pros and cons, but how she feels about the issues. She really searches her insides and can appear to an observer as though she is standing still. That is far from the case. In a relationship, she will explore the same situation or circumstance from many different parts of herself. If her inside process were explicit, it would sound something like this: "How do I feel about your decision to change jobs when I am in this mood? How do I feel about it when I am in other moods? One part of me feels good about it—let's see what that is about. Another part of me feels another way—let's explore than, etc., etc." When you follow her process, it may look as though she is not getting anywhere in her growth attempt. It is only when you look back over time that you realize how far she has moved. Her lover is not yet fully in touch with his insides to be clear about his basic rhythm yet. For this reason, they are both unsure about whether or not they will stay together. It is clear, however, that for her maximum satisfaction in a relationship she needs someone whose rhythm is similar to her own. Otherwise, she will always be frustrated in her exploration.

The concept of rhythm in human development and relationships is based on a view of the human organism as an energy system—flowing and moving, never static—controlled by energy, fed by energy, directed by energy, and with the ability to connect with other people and things in the external environment via energy as well as touch, taste, smell, sight, and sound. The more in tune an individual feels with himself as an energy flow, the more in touch or at one he feels with his outside environment. Many people have achieved this experience momentarily with drugs. Some drugs inhibit and reduce the external controls and thought processes so that the individual is left with heightened sensory apparatus. He may get in touch with feelings he has been repressing which scare or upset him so badly he cannot experience much else. However, if that does not happen, he will begin to get a sense of himself as a flowing organism, in touch with the flow of the world around him. People use drugs for many different reasons, of course. However, I have seen a number of people who have used them for this purpose—to get in touch with that inner part of themselves which I have described as basic rhythm. I have found, though, that when an individual begins to get in touch with his natural rhythm via the growth processes I have mentioned, he learns to respect and appreciate it rather than fight it (i.e., fit his environment into his rhythm as much as possible rather than the other way around). Then he can experience a turn-on far beyond where any drug can take him. I am convinced that the individual's own inner mechanism, once activated and operating freely without interference, is capable of far greater potential for aliveness than most people have ever dreamed of experiencing. When rhythm is understood and experienced by two people, the focus of any relationship changes from protection, security, or rescue to one of enhancing that kind of aliveness. It is a reality that two free-flowing energy systems, together and in touch, produce sparks, static, and power in geometric progression.

Connections can fail to work for other reasons besides rhythm differences. There may be discrepancy in life-style, rule structure for relationships, and nature of commitment.

An individual's life-style is based on the many parts of himself, including his rhythm, his choice of work, his eating and sleeping preferences, his life experience in what he has learned from others, his needs for physical space and for contact with others. You hear jokes about the person who likes to sleep until noon marrying someone who is up and jumping at six a.m. In reality, that is often a difficult adjustment, especially during leisure times like weekends and vacations. However, that difference doesn't usually cause any connection to dissolve. If there are many of those kinds of differences, though, there has to be a great deal of nurturing in the relationship when the two people do connect to make it all worthwhile. Otherwise, they will begin to live more and more separate lives. My experience is that if people have a deep and nurturing relationship when they are together and creative outlets for themselves individually, they can handle differences in life-style, even great differences, with a minimum of stress and disruption. However, if the relationship is faltering in other areas, an additional burden here will often tip the scale. Life-style will become a much more important area of adjustment for couples as women grow in the development of their creativity. In many families now, the wife adjusts her life to fit the husband's life-style. It is much more difficult to work out when each has a definite life-style.

A difference in rule structure can often make a connection impossible even if all other aspects of the connection are ideal. For example, the requirements that some religious sects make for their members are often experienced as very intrusive by a spouse who does not share the religious belief. No matter how understanding or considerate each person is there may be some aspect of the individual's involvement in the religion that creates constantly escalating resentment in the other. This is true particularly if the individual's rule structure, based on his religion, is really basic to his life-style. Many religious groups are really a subculture, a whole way of life. It is risky to assume that any two people ought to be able to adjust just because they have great feeling for each other. I think this understanding is part of the reason Catholics, Mormons, and Jews, for example, prefer their children to marry within the religion.

Other differences in rule structure have to do with moral values. Let us take, for example, a woman who prefers to have a basic, deep relationship with one man but also have sex occasionally with others. She considers marrying a man who believes in sexual faithfulness. Now, they may discuss this and it may be possible for her to go along with his wishes without any problem; or he may be able to tolerate her differentness in this respect as long as she is discreet and doesn't tell him about her experiences. On the other hand, each may agree to the other's demand because he or she wants to please and feels it will work out, but in reality cannot go along without resenting the other. If that is so, I don't know any way to resolve it. I would suspect that if this difference is not resolvable, it is an indication that there is a basic rhythm difference which is not yet apparent to either of them in the relationship.

The commitment area has to do with what is important to each person. When one person's major commitment has to do with home and family—planning for them, doing things together, spending time with each other—and the spouse is committed primarily to his or her work, it can be the origin of constant irritation to both of them. Political and religious differences as well as work choices can be external expressions of major differences as to what is important in life.

The meaning of commitment to each person and the way in which each commits may evoke major differences. Some people connect on the commitment that "I'll stay with you all my life, no matter what happens." Others commit on the basis that "I'll stay with you as long as I have feeling for you, as long as our relationship is rewarding." Such commitments are not often explicit, but become evident by the behavior of both parties. To one person, the way in which he or she follows through on the commitment to stay together may be to share in all the duties, cooperate in making and spending the money, and share responsibility for the children. To another, staying together may mean working on the marital relationship, spending time together, sharing feelings, and growing in the relationship. Some people perceive and honor commitment based on the values of their parents, or of society in general, superimposed on their own lives whether such values fit or not.

In reality, the only honest and humanly feasible commitment two people can make to each other is to follow through on any interaction until all the feelings are out in the open and clear. In other words "I will hear you out, and I know that you will hear all of my feelings on this issue, without seeing our differences as a statement about how much we care for each other; without judging who is right or wrong but with respect for our right to be different, and the courage and respect for our commitment to each other to be honest and clear about who we are." When all the feelings are clear, it may be evident that two people do not fit. However, with this commitment, major decisions about the relationship will not be made in the midst of trauma, impulse, or hurt. Major decisions will be made when everything is out in the open and clear, on real issues about limitations and needs and individual differences. I can say the words "I will love you forever," but I do not have the ability to control how I feel. I can control my behavior, but not my feelings. They change, deepen, or wane regardless of any act of will on my part. My feelings are not subject to my will. This commitment to follow through on feelings in the moment may sound simple. It is far from that—perhaps the most difficult commitment anyone can make—because it is possible and based on reality. Think of how many situations you have experienced where you have left feelings unsaid and either "stewed" about it or regretted it later, and you can begin to understand the depth of that kind of commitment. It is on that commitment that real trust is built. "I know I can rely on you to be honest with me about who you are even when it is painful to both of us. Because I know how difficult it is to be honest about my own feelings, I know how much investment you have in our relationship to make the effort to be honest with me. It is much easier, in the moment, to walk away, to withhold feelings, to repress them. You think you are protecting me, but you are hurting me more this way than by anything you could do or say because you are undermining trust between us and building a barrier I cannot penetrate."

Many times people interpret honesty in a relationship as the absence of privacy. They assume that each must know everything about the other—their whole life history, everything they say and do. I see this kind of revelation as quite separate from the commitment to honesty I am talking about. What each reveals to the other, I think is entirely a matter of what fits the individual's personal preference and comfort. The commitment to honesty essential to the growth of the relationship has to do with being open about all the feelings connected to who I am and to the relationship. In other words "You will know when I am hurt, unhappy, warm, relaxed, worried, or afraid. I will also take responsibility for saying no to you when I don't want something or don't like something; and I will let you know my needs and my demands. If you will do the same, then on this basis we can make room in our relationship for each of us to grow and enhance the other." It is a joy in a relationship to be a part of someone else's growth as well as to experience your own. This commitment to emotional honesty and growth lays the base for the deepest form of connection between male and female.

Chapter Eleven:

The Intimate Connection

I believe that the deepest kind of intimacy possible between two human beings requires, as a base, that each person feel he is a separate whole person who wants to love and share, but who knows, without question, that he can survive emotionally alone. The individual can then be completely open to the self-expression of his partner; yet, not in any way dependent on such expression from the other for his own continuing emotional survival. Without this base, it is impossible to see the other person as he really is. He or she is seen "as I want him to be, as a judge, as responsible for me in some way, as my Saviour." The individual must accept that no one can really take him over—control him—and that he is really unable to take over or control anyone else. He takes the risk for the determination, expression, and evolution of what is fitting for himself and uses that determination as his basis for functioning and for direction in his life. He manifests his internal processes (thoughts, feelings, sensations, perceptions, cognitions, assumptions, and conclusions) clearly and congruently. His assertions are characterized by authenticity, spontaneity, integrity, courage, and the kind of commitment that involves the acceptance of responsibility for one's own total emotional honesty. The price involved in such separateness and commitment is the possibility of not connecting with some particular person, and the pain when this occurs. The real risk in not connecting is momentary loneliness and isolation. The illusory risk we often operate on is that "If I lose you, there is a death in a part of me." The experience of deep intimacy, then, is connected to the individual's ability to assert who he is and to experience aloneness without associating the experience with death. Thus, the sense of autonomy requires that the individual learn ways of expressing his true self that give him the certainty he can relate to and get from others without having to prostitute or distort himself; and that the individual feel certain of survival at times when he doesn't make connections. The payoff for this kind of autonomy and commitment to self is maximum development of the individual's creativity and the deepest possible experience of human interaction when the individual does connect.

Many people misunderstand when I talk about autonomy and commitment to self. They see an image of a spoiled brat blithely demanding that everyone do everything his way—if they don't give him what he wants then "the hell with them." This is far from the truth. The reality is that the commitment is twofold: to present self as clearly and honestly as possible without apology or defense; and to express that self to others without judging, depreciating, or intruding upon them. I think this concept can best be understood by example. The following is an excerpt of dialogue from a treatment session with a couple who are making the shift into separateness and clear presentation of self:

Therapist: Have there been any changes in the bedroom?"

Wife: Well, yes—I was a tiger last night. I have never done that before. I always let him take the lead.

Husband (*smiling, looking pleased*): I liked that— it surprised me, but it was nice.

Therapist: Did you have any mixed feelings? Usually people do when they make a change, even if it is a change they want and like.

Wife: Well, I felt like I was manipulating him, like if I am nice to him, he will do anything I want.

Therapist: Where did you get the idea he was such a patsy? Is it a familiar feeling to you to manipulate others?

Wife: Yes, I manipulated both of my parents. I was a good girl with my mother, always doing the right thing and then doing what I really wanted behind her back, constantly playing tricks on her to keep her from finding out. I think she pretended not to know—as long as I played the game on the surface, it was OK. My father I could wheedle, smile, tease him and he gave me what I wanted. If I came out with what I really felt, he would "turn me off."

Husband: I think you are phony sometimes, telling me what you think I want to hear.

Therapist (*to wife*): You don't seem to want to manipulate any more. I can see that it feels depreciating to you. You did it to survive as a child and it worked, but it is defeating you now. However, it is very hard to shift that way of operating.

Therapist (*to husband*): If your wife starts coming out straight, that means you won't always like what you hear, but when you do connect it will be stronger and more exciting. Can you accept that kind of change?

Husband: I could not have before. If she did not give me something I really wanted, I would have thought she didn't love me. Now, I realize that only means she is at a different place inside herself, and if I want the best of her I have to take the parts I don't like so well also.

Therapist *(sees wife looking tenderly at husband)*: What do you want to do?

Wife: I want to touch him. *(They hold hands and look at each other.)*

Therapist: Now, tell each other what you feel inside.

Wife: There are times when I feel very angry with you and I don't say anything.

Husband: I want you to tell me how you feel. I want to know.

Therapist *(to both)*: You have been living with a myth, that the expression of anger or the assertion of yourself in some way the other doesn't like is destructive. The reality is that anger or differentness can be the route to some of the most beautiful experiences in marriage if you learn to express it in ways that keep the connection open to you.

When two people who experience themselves as separate and autonomous meet and are attracted to each other, they immediately begin the process of expressing who they are. Each has a tacit, perhaps even out-of-awareness commitment to self which determines his or her behavior. If it were explicit, the commitment would go something like this: "I will not hide myself from you to impress you, to keep you from getting upset or to keep from disappointing you. Neither will I deliberately try to upset you or disappoint you or keep from impressing you. My way of presenting myself is based on expressing me congruently and clearly so that I can feel good about myself and you can get a clear picture of who I am. Perhaps I find that I like you and I would like you to like me. But if you do not like me or I do not fit with you in some way, I would just as soon know about it rather than

waste my time. My worth is not dependent on whether or
not you like me. It is connected to whether or not I am
straight and clear about myself. Each time I honor what I feel
openly and congruently, I add a notch to my self-esteem. In
addition, each time I act on what I feel, I open myself up to
additional feelings I may not know I had. It becomes a
self-perpetuating process. My growth becomes dependent on
my consistently honoring my insides by my words and
actions. That may occasionally create crises for me, may lose
me a friend sometimes, but I am convinced I can achieve my
best growth and connections out of who I really am. I act on
faith and experience that that is better than anything I can
pretend to be."

Therefore, the first step toward an intimate connection is
for each person to reveal himself as he really is without
letting the possibility of another's judgment deter him.

Again an example:

Wife: I can't say how I feel because then you will tell
me what a bitch I am and how bad I am . . .
Therapist: He is in charge of whether or not you are
OK?
Wife: Well, actually, that is so—it's very important to me
what he thinks.
Husband: I feel the same way. It is painful to me when
you tell me I am not a man and you don't respect me. I
try to please you all the time, and nothing seems to be
good enough.
Therapist: Her response determines how you come out
with your feelings?
Husband: What's wrong with that? I am sure this is the
case in 75 percent of American marriages; most hus-
bands try to please their wives and American women are
becoming very demanding . . .
Therapist (interrupting): Let's bring in the troops!

Husband *(to therapist)*: Well, you can make fun of me, but just ask . . .

Therapist: It isn't my intent to make fun of you. I am trying to get you to see what is happening. You are trying to make contact with each other, and it is coming out as if each of you is helpless—the other is in charge of you and you can bring in the "legal briefs," the "statistics" and the "jury" to prove it! All your evidence may prove you are absolutely right, so where does that leave you? If you pursue this way of getting in touch, one of you always has to lose, to be one down. When that happens, both of you really lose.

Another example:

Husband *(to wife)*: You are always taking care of things in the family, always in control, never trusting me . . .

Wife: I would like to be able to trust you but you always let me down.

Husband: It is true that I have let you down often in the past, but I am trying to change that." *(Looks down and slouches.)*

Therapist: I notice that you start to come out with how you feel to your wife, she responds, and then you sort of "fold up."

Husband: I start to feel guilty. I really don't want to hurt her.

Wife: It doesn't throw me as much for you to tell me how you feel as it does for you to "fold up."

Therapist *(to husband)*: Do you believe that?

Husband: Yes, I guess so . . .

Therapist: OK, let's go back—what makes you fold up?

Husband *(talks softly, head hanging)*: I guess I'm afraid she'll stop giving to me.

Therapist: She's a good mama.

Wife: I don't want to be his mother.

Therapist *(to wife)*: So, how come you keep taking over?

Wife: I guess I have always been the one who was there when the chips were down. I always took care of everybody else's feelings; taking over is all I know.

Therapist: In different ways, both of you felt very lonely as children—no one really heard or took care of your feelings. *(to husband)* Your mother, from what you have said before, took good care of you physically as long as you didn't cross her. So, perhaps being given to is connected in your insides with not asserting yourself.

Husband: That's true. She was a good cook, she was always there when I was sick, she kept my clothes cleaned and ironed, but she would not let me have a thought of my own.

Therapist *(to wife)*: No one took care of you physically or emotionally. If you begin to let your husband take care of some of your feelings now, you have to give up being the "Big Mama," always in control—that's scary. *(Wife starts to cry.)*

When a therapist works with a marital pair, he or she is really working with six people—the people in front of him and the parental "ghosts" behind each of them. All of us have a difficult time sometimes being autonomous and separate and staying in the present with each other because we are still not separated completely from our parents. We sometimes project on to our spouses perceptions and expectations connected more with early family experiences rather than with the present relationship. Our focus in therapy is always on the current relationship, and we move in and out between past and present as the process of growth in therapy takes us. As the past emerges, we deal with that in attempting to understand its meaning for translation back to the present. So, the treatment is a flowing process just as any relationship is a flowing process; and the understanding and use of the past as a way of deepening and better understanding our present is a useful process for all of us in our continuing growth, and not just peculiar to therapy. Growth is an unfolding process, flowing back and forth between past, present, and future. In the growth process, time has no boundaries. In any given moment, we are living in the past, present, and future at the same time.

The second step in building the base for an intimate connection is for one partner, the husband for example, to view what the other has to offer as a statement about her—what she likes, what she doesn't like, what she wants, what her limitations are—rather than as a statement about him. Therefore, if she doesn't like the same things he likes or doesn't want to go everywhere he wants to go, that has nothing to do with whether or not she cares about him or approves of him or wants to be with him. If the wife expresses sad feelings, the husband can hear her feelings without thinking, he has failed or she wouldn't be sad. If the husband expresses some hope for the future, his wife can listen to his hopes without assuming, that means he isn't satisfied with her because if he were "he wouldn't be talking about growth and change."

For example:

Husband: Things have been pretty hectic this week—a lot has been going on.
Therapist: You seem low to me.
Husband: Low?
Therapist: Sad, somehow. Your posture is slouched, your expression is somewhat sad, your tone is low.
Husband: Well, I am tired, I've been busy . . .
Wife: Well, Tom died Wednesday, it was sudden. You haven't said much, but I'm sure it upset you.

Husband: Oh, yes. *(Aside to Therapist)* Tom was a good friend my age I have known for twenty years. *(Changes subject.)* Also, our daughter went to camp this weekend . . .

Therapist *(interrupting)*: You shifted very quickly from Tom. You must have had lots of feelings about that. Could you respond to your wife's offer to hear your feelings?

Husband *(glances at wife, then down)*: Well, it did hit me pretty hard. It was so sudden, made me think of my own death . . .

Therapist: I notice you are talking to your wife, but not looking at her.

Husband *(looks up with tears in eyes)*: I don't know why I am doing this—I never cry.

Therapist: I don't understand that.

Husband: *(Puts head in hands and begins to sob.)*

Therapist *(to wife)*: Your husband is giving you a gift of his feelings and you seem very far away—what are you feeling?

Wife: I have never seen him like this—it frightens me . . .

Therapist: Could you share that with him? Would you look at each other and share that? *(They look at each other.)*

Wife: I have never seen you cry before. It frightens me like something bad is happening.

Husband: I don't feel bad, it feels good, like a relief—like I have been holding it in for a long time.

Therapist *(to wife)*: Could you explore further with your husband what his tears mean to you? *(to husband)* Could you listen and hear her words as an effort on her part to understand herself and you and not as a criticism of you?

Husband: I think so.

Wife: I always want you to be strong. I guess tears mean weakness to me, yet I don't really feel that way. People should cry if they feel like it. My father could cry, but I did not respect him very much—I never felt I could depend on him.

Therapist *(to wife):* Maybe you made a connection between those two facts when there really isn't one.

Wife *(to husband):* I never thought of that. You are dependable, you have never really let me down; I am sorry if I have kept you from expressing to me what you really feel.

Husband: I guess I thought it was weak to cry, too—my father was a stoic, a good man, but the strong, silent type.

Therapist *(to both):* So, we have made a discovery; the expression of feeling, no matter what the feeling is, is a strength rather than a weakness and the road to understanding and profound contact between husband and wife.

This couple is learning to express their feelings and to hear the other's expression of feeling in a nonjudgmental acceptance, receiving the feeling as the gift of contact. You have to care about the relationship to take the trouble to express to someone what you really feel. It is not easy to communicate deep feeling.

The third step toward an intimate connection is to view differentness and disagreement as an opportunity for growth and understanding rather than as a put-down or criticism; and to present differentness or disagreement as a statement about self and not a judgment or criticism of the other person. In this way, people can differ without a feeling of loss to themselves. For example, I see myself as in charge of me and my worth. I do not look to you for approval of what I say, do, or think. Your opinion is important to me and I respect it, but it does not determine my value to me. Therefore, if you tell me there is something you don't like about me, I can afford to look at what you have to say because, while I care about what you like and don't like, the weight of my world isn't hanging on it. I am aware that the way in which I manifest myself may not always clearly express the way I really feel inside. In order for me to keep growing and developing in my ability to express myself, I need responses from you and others about how you see me so that I can constantly check on the congruency between the way I feel and the way I show how I feel. In addition, I may be trying to offer you help in some way; but, the way in which I offer it may seem intrusive to you. I need to know this from you so that, if it is possible for me to do so, I can change the way I offer help so it will fit you better. As long as I am going to give you a gift, I'd just as soon give you something you like. Therefore, when you tell me something you don't like about me, I examine what you express to me and use that information to explore within myself. Perhaps you have seen something I didn't know was there that I would really like to change—i.e., I'm trying to give to you and it's coming out as if I'm pushing you in some way:

Wife: Can I help you with your report? I know you have to have it in by tomorrow.
Husband: Thanks, but it's coming along OK.
Wife: Why don't you let me type it for you—then you can look it over and see what you want to change. That'll save you some time.
Husband: Damn it, will you knock it off! I know you're trying to help, but I'm under pressure to get this done, and you're just interfering.

I may be irritated or momentarily hurt in this exchange, but basically I have learned that if I offer help and you say no, you really mean it. You're just not wanting to be urged. Therefore, I gained something because I have learned something that I can use—I have a tendency to push a little and you don't like to be pushed—and you have gained something in the exchange because you have taught me something about yourself that is important to our relationship.

In another instance, perhaps you have seen something that I may or may not have known about myself before; however, what I am doing fits me and I cannot change it and still be honest about myself. For example:

Husband: Let's have the Johnsons over for dinner tomorrow night.

Wife: I don't want to have the Johnsons over again. We've already had them over three times in the last two months and I can't remember the last time we were there.

Husband: Oh, honey, that's petty. I enjoy the Johnsons.

Wife: I admit it's petty, but that's the way I feel. If we had them over, I'd be uncomfortable and resentful all evening, and I won't do that to myself.

Husband: Well, it irritates me that you feel that way, but I admit I would rather have it this way than have them over and you look grumpy all evening.

In this instance, I may feel sorry that I cannot give you what you want, and you may be annoyed that I feel differently than you; but, each of us has still gained, because you know something about my limitations—what I can and cannot give—and I know something new about what bothers you. In addition, we have been able to share that difference in our feelings about it without exerting force on the other to change his mind by making judgments, threats, cajoling, looking hurt, withholding, or withdrawing. We have respected each other's boundaries. The relationship thus continues to be defined, perhaps with disappointment or irritation at times, but without loss of self-esteem. We continue to enhance each other even though we are differing or denying the other something he wants; and each of us continues to enhance self by functioning on the basis, "I cannot give you everything you want, but I have enough to give to make me and someone else happy without having to force myself or hurt myself by trying to give beyond my limits."

Here's another example of a couple in treatment who are just beginning to consider the possibility of differentness as something positive rather than destructive:

Therapist: What brought you here?

Husband: Well, I am a weakling. I drink periodically. I don't come home when I say I'm going to. I don't always keep my word.

Wife: Oh, he is not as bad as he says, he is always overdoing things. The truth is . . .

Therapist *(to wife)*: You are speaking for him.

Husband: She usually speaks for me, she is more articulate.

Therapist: I don't have any trouble understanding you.

Husband: Well, it is easier to let her talk for me.

Therapist: You don't look happy about it.

Wife: Well, really, doctor, we are here because of our daughter who is taking drugs, and we can't seem to control her.

Therapist: I understand your concern about your daughter, but I do not understand your changing the subject.

Husband: She often changes the subject in the middle of a conversation.

Therapist: Could you say that to her directly and let her know how you feel about that?

Husband *(to wife):* It makes me angry when you change the subject in the middle of a conversation . . .

Wife: Well, darling, I . . .

Therapist *(to wife)*: You are interrupting. *(to husband)* You are letting her interrupt.

Husband: Let me finish. I can never keep my train of thought. You are always off somewhere else. Why don't you stick to one thing?

Wife: Well, I was concerned about our daughter because . . .

Therapist: There you go again.

Wife: What do you mean?

Therapist: Changing the subject. Could you respond to what your husband just said to you?

Wife: What did you say, dear?

Husband: I said, why don't you stick to one thing?

Wife: Well, you know I always have so many things hanging over me, right?

Husband: Right.

Wife: Well, you never seem to be around when I need you—right?

Therapist: You just did it again.

Wife: What?

Therapist: You set him up. Do you notice what is happening? You constantly cut your husband off from expressing himself by talking for him, by presenting him with conclusions—that's the way it is, isn't it dear?—by interrupting him, by telling him he does not mean what he says, by defending yourself and presenting your case instead of exploring his feelings. You, husband, cooperate beautifully in this by withdrawing, agreeing, keeping your feelings to yourself. It is as though the two of you are operating as if you have an agreement not to make any real contact. What are you afraid of?

Husband *(after long pause)*: I'm afraid I could kill her.

Therapist: You are sitting on a lot of anger.

Husband: Yes, all my life.

Therapist: Then part of your anger that has never come

out is connected with your wife and part, perhaps, to your family before her?

Husband: Yes, I used to have temper tantrums when I was a young child. *(Goes into exploration of early difficulty in expressing anger in family.)*

Wife: I have felt this and I am very frightened of it—more that he would leave me if he got angry enough at me.

Therapist: I feel that both of you have many strong feelings that have never come out and that you are frightened of them—that is understandable. If you have never experienced expressing strong feeling in a constructive way, the possibility of doing so seems overwhelming and catastrophic. However, the route to being in charge of your feeling is to let it out and find out it is not as overwhelming as you thought. So, I would like to recommend that you come into a married couples' therapy group. The group makes it possible for you to begin to learn how to express your feelings with others who are not connected so deeply to you, and such learning serves as a bridge to begin expressing to each other. Also, if the expression does get out of hand while you're learning—which it does sometimes in the beginning because it has been building up for so long—there are enough people in the group so that we can exert controls from the outside so you don't have to worry about hurting yourself or someone else.

In order to express differentness, judgment must be removed from the feeling area. Feelings are not right or wrong, good or bad, they are just feelings; and they need to be understood as such so that they can be shared and understood in terms of what the feelings mean in relation to the individual and the relationship. There is a strong element of risk in this—that, as people get in touch with what they really feel, they may really be quite different than they appeared to each other when they first met; or, in the case of the couple in the dialogue, they may be very different than the façades they each showed to the other earlier in the marriage. Therefore, opening up what is really there may mean establishing a very different basis for their relationship, which they may or may not be able to do, and which carries the risk of the possible loss of the relationship. The threat of loss may diminish as a couple defines their relationship over the years, but the process of really confronting someone you care deeply about with your own deepest feelings always seems somewhat risky:—"You may not want me if you see me as I really am." People take that risk because they are striving for the kind of relationship that allows maximum growth for each of them individually and for their interaction with each other.

The fourth step toward an intimate connection is the commitment on the part of each person to work through whatever emerges until all the feelings are out in the open and clear. Everything—all the issues—does not always have to be resolved or compromised or agreed upon for a relationship to work well. Often, there are differences that come up that are not resolvable and, while it may be painful that we can't come to a decision agreeable to both of us, it often isn't really catastrophic. However, for the relationship to grow, all the feelings have to be resolved—not agreed with but expressed and heard and understood—so that neither partner is carrying "excess baggage" in his insides in the form of resentment, hurt, or even tenderness and longing; and, so that each is validated by his partner's hearing and respecting his feelings. The commitment on the part of both is, "I cannot in any honesty commit myself to love you all of my life. I cannot control or predict how I will continue to feel. I can only honestly commit myself to follow through with you on whatever comes up between us." That does not imply a literal contract to follow through in a certain way. Each individual has his own rhythm for handling disagreements. Some people start marriage with a rule that neither can go to bed angry. That doesn't make sense in that it may not fit the situation or the feelings involved or the individual rhythm. One individual may have to go to bed angry and come out with his feelings the next day. If he had to follow this rule, he would have to stay up all night. The commitment is not toward a particular way—it is toward a process. The process is that in his own way and time, he or she will take responsibility for expressing himself and will hear the other out. Often, when all the feelings and issues are out in the open and clear, decisions tend to evolve. They do not have to be made in the sense that each individual logically weighs all the pros and cons. When the feelings are clear and each person knows his own and the other's limitations and needs, it becomes clear what must be done and in what way. Here is an example of a couple beginning to explore the nature of this kind of commitment.

Husband: I am really pissed off at you. You treat me like a little boy. I try to tell you what I feel and you, in effect, pat me on the head like I haven't got good sense. I am sick and tired of it.

Wife: *(Sits with hands folded primly and smiles benignly.)*

Therapist (to wife): Your husband is coming out with some real feeling, but I don't get any message from you about what you are feeling inside.

Wife: Well, he is probably right.

Therapist: Well, that wraps that up!

Wife: There's no point in both of us getting mad.

Therapist: What would happen?

Wife: No one would be in control.

Therapist: What is the worst that would happen?

Wife: He would hit me.

Husband: I did hit you but that was three years ago—I can change.

Therapist *(to wife)*: Do you believe that?

Wife: Maybe, but I am still afraid . . .

Therapist: What is the fear—what is your worst phantasy—let's pretend . . .

Wife *(begins to cry)*: I will be alone and no one will hear me.

Therapist: Your husband is listening. Hold his hand and tell him about the loneliness. *(to husband)* Try to listen to your wife's feelings without feeling as though you have to do something for her. Just listen and try to stay in touch with your own feelings.

Wife *(to husband)*: It's like when I was little and I would hide in my room and hear my mother and father fighting. He would beat her up and she would be screaming. Then he would leave the house and stay away for days. One day he did not come back. *(She begins to sob deeply, husband takes her in his arms.)*

Therapist *(to both)*: Maybe you can't promise each other that you will be there always, or even that you will love each other always. However, you can make a commitment to each other that you will stay with each other until feelings are resolved. It isn't the leaving or even the hitting that is the most destructive thing. It is that both these acts may cut off contact and leave people hanging with their feelings, so that the expression of feeling becomes synonymous with abandonment and violence. The reality is that if people can learn to handle their own and the feelings of others in a fitting way, there may be separation, but there is never abandonment or violence.

In these dialogue examples I have been offering, you will notice that we don't talk much about content like sex, money, religion, children and all the issues people fight about. That does not mean that these issues do not come up or have ceased to be important; it only means that they are just the vehicles around which people express their feelings and attempt to make contact. As therapists, we do not focus on the issues. People can resolve issues easily enough if they are in touch with how they really feel about those issues and if they are able to express their differences to each other in a way that separates the differences from whether or not they love each other. Our focus then is on the growth processes people use for making contact. I see therapy as making explicit the old, defeating, lethal processes and teaching new ones. We do not change people—although people do change, often drastically, as a result of letting go of destructive processes and adopting new ones which enhance the uniqueness of each in his own eyes and those of the other. The focus is not on outcome, resolution, or results—the focus is on contact. "How can I let my insides be in touch with your insides, whatever emotional state each of us is in?" That contact is really what is most satisfying. The human dilemma is how to assuage loneliness without destroying individual uniqueness and creativity; how to soar in exploration of each person's creative difference without producing isolation and its accompaniment—despair.

The fifth step in an intimate connection is the acceptance on the part of both that we cannot change feelings by an act of will; that each must be in charge of establishing his own boundaries so that he does not give to the point of resentment. It is no gift to you for me to agree with you or give you what you want if I will resent doing it. One way or another, you will be aware of the resentment. I cannot hide it. It will come out in ways I am not even aware of. Swallowed resentment has a thousand devious expressions. I will agree to do something and then forget to do it or put it off, with very reasonable excuses for having done so, of course. I will begin to feel irritable much of the time without knowing why and tend to overreact to small difficulties. I may become slightly withdrawn and less responsive than usual; and I may become cold, unresponsive or impotent sexually—the most insidious way of expressing unresolved resentment. Therefore, I may be giving in to save our relationship and not rock the boat, but I am, without question, destroying the relationship—just doing it more slowly. If I come out with my feelings and say no, there is a chance we won't fit with each other, but there is also a chance for a deep, free, and honest connection. If I don't hold to my boundaries and give in, there is no chance at all. We may stay together, but with much unspoken resentment between us, we won't have much of a relationship. Therefore, it is a real gift from me to you for me to say no to you and take your open irritation and disappointment at being denied something you want. I am doing you no favor by saying yes to you and then taking out my resentment in indirect ways I may not even be aware of, and with which you have no way of dealing because they are indirect and devious.

Here is an example of the insidious nature of resentment grown out of infringement on individual boundaries:

Husband *(to wife)*: I am suddenly aware that I am not really happy with what I am doing at work, but I don't know what I really want to do either. I feel depressed and immobilized much of the time. *(to the Therapist)* I am even impotent with my wife. I know this is frustrating to her and I feel guilty about that.

Wife: I feel as though you leave me hanging, like I really do not want sex with you if you are going to get me aroused and then just not follow through.

Husband: You sound as though I do it deliberately; I just can't help it!

Therapist *(to husband, burlesquing)*: Poor baby!

Husband *(to therapist)*: I do feel helpless . . .

Therapist *(to husband)*: Look at your wife and say to her, "I am helpless like a little baby."

Husband *(looking at wife)*: I am helpless—goddamn it, I am not helpless! I am just sick and tired of your control and your demands and your endless bitching about what I don't do right. I feel like my mother ran my life until I married you, and you have run it ever since.

Therapist *(to husband)*: Whose responsibility is that?

Husband: Mine. I am responsible for my life.

Therapist *(to husband)*: Could you look at your wife and say that to her?

Husband *(looking at wife)*: I am responsible for my life and for what I do. *(looks intently at wife)* You know it really does not have to do with you that I feel controlled and helpless. I invite you to step in and take over.

Wife: I know I do it, but I really don't want to control you anymore . . .

Therapist *(to husband)*: Do you believe that?

Husband: Yes, I think I really do. But I am afraid to take responsibility for myself. What happens if I begin to do what I feel and to take some risks to act on my feelings—what if I make an ass of myself?"

Therapist: Yes, what would be so bad about that?

Husband: I don't know, nothing I guess . . .

Therapist: What is the worst that could happen?

Husband *(looking at wife)*: She would leave me . . .

Therapist: Could you check that out with her, how she feels . . .

Wife: I would be afraid, I'm not used to you telling me what you really feel; but I think anything would be better than having you resent me the way you do. I feel so far away from you—it's almost worse than being alone . . .

Therapist: So both of you are frightened because you're going into new territory—taking the risk to learn how to express to each other your real needs and limitations. It takes much courage to begin a new journey like this because you don't know where it will lead you. All you know is that you cannot continue the way you have been operating because it is too painful and destructive to you. So, you're taking the risk on faith that you might be able to work out a better, more satisfying way of connecting.

The sixth step toward an intimate connection is for both individuals to be clear in stating their boundaries, and for each to hear the other's boundaries as limitations and needs not as ultimatums or attempts to control. For example:

Husband: You asshole! You acted like a real bitch with George—when it gets to the point where I can't even bring my friends around . . .
Wife: Shut up! I'm willing to listen to how you feel, but when you call me names something inside of me freezes up and I can't hear anything after that. I've got too much respect for me to let you or anyone else call me names.
Husband: That's too bad about you . . .
Wife: If you keep calling me names, you're setting it up so that I can't hear you—is that what you want?
Husband: OK, OK, I hear you, I hear you . . .

She's saying to him very clearly that she can't fight with name-calling. Some people can—it probably wouldn't bother him if she reciprocated by calling him names. However, that doesn't fit her. She is saying, "I'm willing to take your heat, but the name calling closes me off. I can't control that, I can only recognize and honor my limit in that respect. It's your name whether or not you want to reach me. If you do, the ng has to go."

Another example:

Wife (*in the middle of a heated argument*): I hate
you! (*Slaps him.*)
Husband: Knock it off! I can't stand it when somebody
hits me—I see red! I don't want to beat you up and I
don't want to walk out, but I'll have to leave if you do
that again because I can't control myself and I'd hate
myself if I hit you!

He's saying to her that she infringes on his personal boundaries when she lashes out at him physically in anger. This isn't
true of everyone. Some couples fight physically as a way of
expressing themselves and it isn't at all destructive to the
relationship. However, individual boundaries are very different and may not have anything to do with logic or ex-
periential learning. They may just have to do with the
individual's natural rhythm and innate sense of himself.

Another example of boundaries concerns the reality that I
have to be in charge of whether or not I am in a place inside
myself that I can hear you. If I am upset about other things
or not feeling well or simply lethargic, I must let you know
that I need to just be with me right now. If I don't honor my
limitations at that moment and try to be in two places at the
same time—concerned with my own upset and at the same
time trying to hear you—you will feel that you do not have
my total attention and feel depreciated or invalidated. If I let
you know that I cannot be with you or hear you at that
moment, you may be disappointed or upset, but you will also
trust that when I am there for you you can rely on my being
totally "there."

I need to know when I get through to you so that you hear
my feelings, and when I do or say something that shuts you
off. If I can change the way I come across so that it reaches
you and still expresses me honestly and clearly, I will do it. I
am concerned with being clear about me, but I am equally
concerned about connecting with you.

The seventh step toward an intimate connection is the clear, internal understanding and acceptance of the fact that neither of us intends to hurt the other. I may hurt you because I do not do what you want or because I do something that irritates or disappoints you. If I can change that without hurting me, I will do it. All you have to do is ask. You don't have to give me a reason, manipulate, or cajole. My giving to you is not dependent on the way in which you ask. It is dependent on my ability to give what you want and on my limitations. If I cannot give you what you ask without hurting me, I take responsibility for that limitation, even though you are very disappointed. I know that if I hurt myself to give to you, I will build resentment within myself that I will not be in charge of, and which will eventually destroy our connection. We are only fooling ourselves if we think we can really connect on some other basis than on who we actually are. Therefore, what I do or refuse to do may cause you hurt, but I do not intend to hurt you. I do what I do to express me. If I cannot find a way to express me that does not hurt you, then you and I cannot connect, not because we don't love each other and aren't willing to give, but because we don't fit. I know it is possible to love someone very much and not fit.

For example, I am a man who has chosen a line of work that I love, that enables me to feel most alive, that I would want to do even if I weren't getting paid for it. Say it involves much traveling away from home, like a salesman, or danger, like an airline pilot or racing-car driver. You, my wife, knew about my dedication to my work when you married me and thought you could live with it. However, as the children came along, you got more and more unhappy about my work because it keeps me away from home, and you need me; or, because with the increasing responsibilities of the family, you become more frightened about losing me. Intellectually, you say to yourself that you knew what I did when we married and, when I'm at home I'm attentive and responsive. Or, if I am in dangerous work, you tell yourself the odds on my getting killed are really slim. No matter how you try to convince yourself, you get more and more irritable, less responsive, more anxious and depressed. Your insides are saying to you, "No matter how much you love him or what reasons you give yourself, you cannot live with this arrangement without hurting yourself irreparably." As your husband, I see this, and I do not want to lose you either, so I change jobs. I try my best to find something I will like—I may even try several different jobs; but although everything seems to be going well on the surface of our lives, I develop a case of exzema all over my body. With the doctor's help, I finally get that cleared up; but not long after I develop pains in my chest and shortness of breath. I think I'm having a heart attack, so I go in for a battery of tests and a thorough examination. There is nothing physically wrong with me that they can find. Reassured, I go on with my life and feel all right for awhile. Then, suddenly and for no apparent reason, the "attacks" start again. This time, the doctor refers me to a psychiatrist. He and I explore the different areas of my life and the conflict about my work comes to light. He warns me that my body is talking to me with these symptoms and telling me that I have myself in a trap. I cannot live with the compromise I have made. If I continue to try to do it, I stand a chance of developing a real heart attack—my body is warning me.

Often, couples are able to compromise about situations like this, with some loss to themselves, but without destruction. However, it isn't uncommon that in some instances compromise is not possible. Many unresolvable issues can be faced and accepted; but some cannot. Sometimes, to try to please another person at the expense of yourself is a life and death choice. This couple may have to face that they cannot give each other what the other one needs in order to survive

and grow within the relationship, not because there is anything wrong with either of them, but because, in a vital area,
their needs are contradictory. It's comparable to the body
apparatus—you can live without an appendix, but not without a liver. Some needs, while important, are luxuries in the
relationship; some needs are necessary to the maximum
flowering and growth of the relationship, but not to its
survival; other needs are vital to the life and growth of the
individuals in the relationship so he or she has no choice but
to honor them.

In another example, husband and wife have two small
children. The wife stayed at home until both of them were in
school and then she went back to work. She is an accomplished legal secretary, who takes great pride in her work and
loves the experience and stimulation of being out in the
business world. Her husband, on the other hand, misses
having her at home when he gets there, with dinner prepared
and a martini waiting. He resents her coming in tired and as
bushed as he is, not able to give to him. Both of them see
that the children would prefer her to a baby-sitter after
school. She could stay home until the children are much
older and find some other creative outlets for herself for part
of the day without hurting herself to the point of serious
loss. However, if she chooses to do that the whole family will
pay a price in that she will not feel as alive, spontaneous,
responsive, and serene as she would if she were doing what
she really wants to do. The husband could tolerate her
continuing to work at this point if he knows it is that
important to her, without resenting it to the point of seriously disturbing himself or the relationship. However, again the
family will pay some price in that, periodically, he will feel
unduly pressured and not as well taken care of as he would
like to be, so there will be occasional outbursts on his part to
"clear the air." What is important is that in this instance,
they can work out some compromise either way without

being destructive. However, it is important for both to respect and appreciate that either way they go, there will be some price for all. With that kind of understanding, they can offset the occasional outbursts of dissatisfaction with other moments of appreciation for the efforts they are both making to give and to appreciate each other's gifts.

The eighth step toward an intimate connection is to accept that "our intent is to give all we can to each other." I will extend myself for you in ways I don't particularly want to; or I may, at your request, give up things I'm not happy about giving up if it is important to you. However, I will not do either of these things if it will hurt me to do it, and hurt is determined by whether or not my action produces continuing, unresolvable, smoldering resentment in me. That kind of resentment is an indication I am going beyond my boundaries; it is a statement that I accept I am not good enough for you and I must be good enough, so I will do what I cannot really do. No connection is possible based on that kind of depreciating process. We can connect with change or compromise, but not with loss to our self-esteem. Therefore, with that understanding about my boundaries, I will reach out and extend myself to please you because you are important to me. We each assume then, that the intent of the other is to give everything we want that is possible for him or her to give, within the framework of his boundaries; therefore, if it looks as though the other is not giving, there is some other reason for this besides a lack of desire to give. He may not be able to, he may be upset over something else, he may not feel well, he may be preoccupied. With that assumption, we make room for each of us to be in a non-giving place without being labeled bad or uncaring.

Chapter Twelve:

The Bond of Trust

With two autonomous separate individuals as a beginning, these eight steps then lay the base for their connection—the foundation and the basic framework for the "house" they are going to live in together. Out of the exploration of themselves and each other within the framework of that structure, a bond begins to develop between them which moves the relationship to a new depth. That bond is intangible, cannot be seen or touched or expressed concretely, but it is strong and tensile like fine steel. That bond consists of a basic trust, the elements of which are:

A. We trust that each of us is giving freely, at any given time, whatever we are capable of giving, based on our abilities, our limitations, and the emotional state we are in at that time. Therefore, there is no need for "measuring" between us—you do this if I do that, etc.—no need for doubt about whether either of us is being had or used. Neither of us has to withhold to protect self; we can let go and let our giving and receiving flow freely without fear.

B. We trust each other for the gift of contact and the commitment to contact. In the midst of a quarrel, while one part of me is furious with you another part of me is appreciating that you are being honest with me about yourself and that I can count on you for that. That means I can let go into my anger and trust you to hear me and to take care of yourself; then I can experience the full force of my feelings because I don't have to worry about you. We can each let go into the full exhilaration of intense feeling and trust each other to ride it through. The reality is that if you tell me where you are inside, even though you are saying something that is disappointing or irritating to me you are doing it to stay in contact with me, to keep barriers of unresolved feeling from building up. If you don't tell me what you feel, to keep from hurting or upsetting me, you will automatically create a barrier between us. I cannot let go into my feeling if I cannot trust you to let me know when I have intruded on you or hurt you. I want to make contact with you, to let you know about me and to find out about you, to experience my feeling to the fullest, because in that experience is my sense of aliveness and my greatest impetus toward growth.

C. We both trust that we can spontaneously come out at any time with anything we feel and there will be room for error. Neither of us will immediately assume that the other intends to hurt, doesn't care, is bad or wrong. If it looks as though you are being intrusive, hurtful, judgmental, or uncaring, I will first assume that something else is going on, because none of those expressions is like you. I will take responsibility for checking out with you what you meant, what your intent was, and where you really are inside before I respond with hurt or disappointment or judgment against you. My first assumption is that you must really be hurting inside if you are coming out in a way that doesn't fit you or that is intrusive or attacking to me.

D. We both trust that "you will hear what I have to say and you will listen to my feelings even if you don't agree with my words or are upset by them." For example:

Wife: Why can't you do what you say you're going to do?

Husband: What do you mean?

Wife: You don't care about me—you never pay attention to my feelings . . . (*voice is rising, chin is trembling, eyes are tearful.*)

Husband (*ignores words, looks as the feeling in her tone and expression—goes over and touches her*): Listen, this isn't like you—what's really the matter?

Wife (*starts crying, lets husband take her in his arms*): I've had such a terrible day—I don't know why I'm taking it out on you—the school called about Johnny, my mother was upset that I forgot her birthday—just one thing after another. Then I looked at that gate you were going to fix and it's still hanging there, and that was the last straw . . .

In this instance, the wife started attacking her husband in her words, but the feeling he perceived coming from her was frustration, panic, helplessness. Because he doesn't see her as some judge over him, he was able to stay with his own feelings instead of leaping into his head with a defensive argument. As he stayed with his feeling, he was able to perceive her on a deeper level than her words and respond on that level. He felt sympathy for her and responded to her feelings with his own rather than trying to deal with her words. Trust deepens and strengthens as we learn to read each other on different levels. We communicate with words, facial expressions, body posture, gestures, tone, nonverbal sounds like grunts and groans. As we begin to learn how to perceive ourselves and each other on all these levels, we are much more apt to respond to the feeling rather than the words. That deepens the trust because it is really on the feeling level that we want to be heard. Who is right or wrong is not important in an intimate connection. It is only important in the courtroom.

In another example:

Wife *(to therapist)*: He came home yesterday and just looked terrible. I tried to help—offered him a drink, asked him to tell me what was wrong; but he just grunted and went off to mow the lawn. Why won't he let me help him?
Husband: *(Looks down; his whole body is in a depressed posture, his face is drawn.)*
Therapist: What makes you think he isn't responding just because he isn't saying words? Look at him, and just see if you can feel his feelings without having to do something about it—just let yourself feel where he is and your own feelings in response.
Husband: I guess I just didn't want to be with anyone yesterday. It was too much effort to tell you that—I just felt so low . . .
Wife: *(Starts to respond verbally.)*
Therapist: Try not to talk for a little. Just look at each other, feel each other's feelings and your own—reach out or respond in any way you want, or just stay with your feelings, but don't talk.

(Husband and wife look at each other for a long moment; then he goes over, sits beside her on the floor and puts his head in her lap. She starts to caress him.)

Therapist: For a moment, try not to take care of him. Just use the physical contact you are now experiencing with each other to savor your own feelings before you go into any action. Learn how to use contact with each other to go deeper inside of yourself.

(Husband and wife sit quietly for a while.)

Therapist: Now, share with the other what each of you is feeling within yourself.

Wife: I feel very warm, like liquid butter inside.

Husband: I feel very relaxed—my head is "turned off"— I'm just aware of a kind of pleasant numbness like just before I go to sleep. . . .

Therapist: Each of you is now experiencing that it is possible to give without having to extend yourself at all, just by being with yourself and letting the other one feel you and himself in contact with you. There are many dimensions of giving. They do not all entail effort. The most valuable gift we can offer is the gift of our insides—that's a gift we can give away and keep at the same time. In addition, the giving of my inside feelings and the opening up of myself to my feelings promotes growth for me as well as providing a gift for you.

In still another instance:

Wife: Damn you! Why couldn't you get home on time! We're a half hour late already and I promised Marge I'd get there early to help her . . .

Husband: I just couldn't get away from the office any sooner—something came up. I had my secretary call you . . .

Wife: Something always comes up! I'm sick and tired of having to make excuses to people . . .

Husband: I can't change that—there are times when our plans will just have to take second place to my work. But, I'm really sorry you're upset—I know how difficult this is for you—and I feel sorry you're upset, I really do.

In this instance, the husband took a clear stand about his behavior, did not apologize for it or defend it, but he also could recognize and respond to his wife's feelings. Many times it is difficult for people to make the separation between feelings and behavior, or feelings and content. It is as though if I recognize and accept your feeling, that means I'm automatically bad or wrong or it means I have to change what I do or do something for you—i.e., if I hear that you are upset and angry, then I have to accept that I am at fault and I have to change. That's not so at all. It is possible to respond to feeling, as the husband did in the above dialogue, without altering behavior or decisions. Often, in a relationship, when feelings are heard and responded to the issue is really unimportant. In other words, I can tolerate your not always getting home on time if you can hear and respect my feelings about it.

E. Another aspect of the bond is that we both trust that not only will you not try to change me, but you really do not want to change me. Even though there are things about me that you don't like, you recognize they are part of the whole package and you truly appreciate and want the whole package. Therefore, you constantly give me the message in a thousand different ways that you would really not change a hair of my head. That message requires an understanding on the part of both about the nature of each one's flow." For example, you may be annoyed by my occasional pettiness, but you recognize that the other side of that flaw is my ability to give without strings. If I try to curb the pettiness and pretend it isn't there when it emerges, I will automatically curb the giving. They are two sides of the same coin. I have to honor the parts of me I don't like in order to experience the parts of me I do like to the fullest. I may be upset sometimes by your rigidity about some things. On the other hand, I really appreciate your ability to be stable and clear in the face of a storm. I'm aware that those two parts, again, are both two sides of the same coin. So, I may complain, but I don't try to change what I don't like about you because the parts I do like are so important to me.

F. We both trust that each is committed to his own growth. For example, I must feel that I am alive and developing and creating as a person in ways that are fitting and satisfying to me. The greatest gift I can give you is my "aliveness" and I must take responsibility for producing and sustaining that. If I relate to you in such a way that my sense of being alive and growing is dulled, you will feel the burden and the guilt daily. If you are experiencing me as alive and growing as a person, you will also experience yourself as contributing to that aliveness; and, therefore you experience yourself as giving the utmost in human expression. What more can you possibly give to anyone than to enhance his or her aliveness? What more validation can you receive as a human being than the knowledge that you have contributed that gift?

With this structure and this bond of trust, two people can complete every transaction that emerges between them without leftover feelings or loss of self-esteem. It is as though they create, out of their interaction, an entity separate from themselves almost with a life of its own. Two imperfect people can create a perfect process out of which everything can be dealt with and turned into growth. The process is not dependent on outcome: The relationship might continue—strengthen and deepen—or the couple might leave each other, and go separate ways. However, if they move away, they will do so through the process they have built and therefore, neither will feel he or she has failed. They will understand that one or both have brown to a different place where they no longer fit with each other. When the pain and hurt of separation has been expressed and passed, each will feel warmth and gratitude for the connection which helped both of them continue their growth. Even though the relationship could not continue, each used it to learn and grow and therefore experience it as positive. I have seen people use even very painful relationships to promote their individual growth. My experience is that if they could have found an easier way to facilitate their necessary growth, they would have done it. I don't believe people put themselves through very painful situations unless that is the only way they can learn what they need to know.

Chapter Thirteen:

Intimate Exploration

With the establishment of the basic structure and the development of the bond of trust, the relationship moves to the next stage of depth which has to do with the deepest possible exploration of each other's insides and of the possible growth directions for the relationship. The initial basic structure was established via the exploration of individual boundaries, limits, and needs. This exploration is on a deeper, less tangible level. It is an exploration of each other's deeper nature—rhythm, hopes, and dreams; and it occurs on four major levels:

A. The first level is the exploration of each one's perceptions of the other's nonverbal behavior. For example:

Wife: You look "down" today—is anything the matter?

Husband: What do you mean?

Wife: Well, I notice that you seem kind of mopey and your face looks drawn.

Husband: I didn't know it showed. I woke up feeling this way . . .

Wife: Anything I can do?

Husband: No, just give me time to pull myself together.

Or:

Husband: You seem less "bouncy" than usual.

Wife: I feel OK, just a little tired; didn't sleep as well as usual.

Or:

Wife: You seem quieter than usual tonight . . .

Husband: I feel very mellow—you know, like all's right with the world.

Or:

Wife: You look very energetic—you've been running around all evening. Just when I think you're going to light, you're up and doing something else . . .

Husband: I feel very anxious about that report at work tomorrow—maybe I could go over it now and you could give me some feedback.

You can see that a couple would need the bond of trust and a mutual commitment to growth to go into this area of exploration. Otherwise, either could feel criticized or intruded upon. The trust ensures that each will hear the other's observations as an attempt to reach out and understand. The commitment to growth means that each will use the other's observations to explore deeper inside of himself. Notice that the comments are observations about the other's outward expression, not interpretations or judgments. That kind of comment leaves room for the other to really take a look at what he is feeling inside without having to defend or explain himself and without having words put into his mouth by someone else.

As each begins to comment on what he sees, he or she will begin to learn the nuances of the other's external expression; *ꝿᵐᵈ* thus, over time, each will develop understanding of where the other one is inside, without words. In addition, as each hears the comments of the other, he can use that information for his own growth. For example, I may think I feel terrible, but as I am saying this my wife comments that my foot looks like it is kind of tapping under the table and my eyes are sparkling. As I pay attention to my body messages, I realize that while one part of me does feel terrible, another part feels pretty good; so, I have begun to learn that I am more complicated than I thought—there are many parts of me.

B. Another level of exploration has to do with exploring the discrepancies in expression. For example, I tell you I like what you're wearing, but I'm frowning as I say it. When you or I notice this discrepancy, I may then become aware that I really don't like what you are wearing, but I didn't want to say so and hurt your feelings; or, I did like it, but was preoccupied with some problem elsewhere.

Another example:

(Husband and wife are having dinner at a restaurant, talking about selling their house.)

Husband: I guess we really ought to sell the house—it's too much to take care of with both of us working . . .

Wife: Well, I think so—of course, I don't like the place as well as you do—I'll be glad to get out of it.

Husband: I'm wondering whether or not we can get our price, though—it needs a lot of work done on it.

Wife: You know, while we've been talking you have been playing with those sugar cubes, and now it looks like you've built a wall. In fact, the more we talk, the higher the wall gets . . .

Husband *(looks at his sugar-cube wall and laughs)*: I

guess this conversation is hard for me. I really love that house—it's like cutting off my right arm to get rid of it. I didn't want to tell you that because I thought you'd think I didn't want to sell it then. I really do—I feel we have to—it doesn't fit our lives anymore; but I feel very sad about it.

As human beings, we have mixed feelings about almost everything we do. That seems to be part of the human condition and is only an expression of the fact that there are many different parts to us. Discrepancies in our behavior are revelations of parts we sometimes are not even aware of until they are pointed out to us. Exploring the discrepancies can open us up to more of the richness of the varicolored, many-dimensional fabric out of which we are made.

I don't mean to imply in all of this that couples should be on the lookout for every flick of an eyelash so that you feel you're under some kind of microscope with each other. So much time in our lives is caught up with activities and responsibilities that we may not have much energy available for the subtleties. What I am offering, however, is that if there is a hunger for growth and if people want to get the most out of a connection, it is vital to make some time to deal with these processes.

C. The third level of exploration has to do with the education of ourselves to the use of our own inner resources—our "body messages."
For example:

Husband: I felt pretty good until I walked into the house tonight—now I feel terrible. I can't figure out if it's me or if I'm picking up something from you?
Wife: Well, I don't know about you, but I feel lousy!
Or:
Wife: My gut feels very tense right now . . .
Husband: You're getting my message. That's the way I

feel. I've been annoyed at you all day, but I have a hard time coming out with it . . .

Or:

Husband: My neck aches . . .

Wife: Are you trying to tell me I'm a pain in the neck? **Husband:** As a matter of fact, I have been feeling more and more tense. I'm getting tired of your complaining. There's been something wrong ever since we started this trip . . .

Wife: "I didn't realize it was that bad—I guess I'm just not a camper. I shouldn't have tried to come—I'm just spoiling it for everybody else.

Husband: If you hate it this much, I think that's true— why torture yourself and me?—I hate to see you so miserable. I guess that's why I didn't say anything. You were already so miserable, I didn't want to get mad at you on top of everything else . . .

Wife: A good fight would have helped . . .

Husband: Maybe you, but not me.

Wife: How's your neck?

Husband: Better. . . .

Our bodies do send messages, do talk to us if we understand their language. For instance, I have found out via exploration with others, that when I feel tense in my gut I am picking up unexpressed fear. When I get overwhelmingly sleepy, knowing I had enough sleep the night before and can't be this tired, I know I'm picking up anger. When the feelings come out into the open, I feel fine. Body language consists of physical sensation and imagery (mental pictures or flashes); states like restlessness, agitation, lethargy; and atmospheric messages, like walking into a board meeting at work and suddenly feeling buoyant, when the mood is good— or like going to a party and suddenly feeling glum when you walk into the room, sensing that the group is low-key and dull. Dr. Frederick Perls, the late eminent founder of Gestalt Therapy, once stated, in effect, that most of us function on less than 10 percent of our human potential—we only use our heads (logic and reasoning ability).

D. The fourth level of exploration has to do with the use of our phantasies and daydreams.

For example:

Husband: What is your idea of the perfect mate?

Wife: Oh, no you don't! I'm not going to fall into *that* trap!

Husband: No, seriously, pretend—what's your dream?

Wife: Let's see. *(Closes eyes.)* I see a limousine stopping, you and I getting out—you in a tuxedo, me in white furs and satin . . .

Husband: You wish we had money?

Wife: Well, I'm not sure that's what it is . . . *(Still has eyes closed.)*

Husband: You want excitement?

Wife: Yes, that's partly it—as I look at that picture, I feel—well, kind of exultant. Everyone is looking at us, we're both preening . . .

Husband: Let's do it!

Wife: Are you out of your mind? We can't afford anything like that!

Husband: No, I mean let's pretend right now. Let's play it out and have a dialogue and see if anything is behind that picture . . .

Wife: That seems kind of silly . . .

Husband: What have we got to lose? There's nobody else around to laugh.

Wife: Why not.

(Both get up—he pretends to get out of the car, leans over to take her hand, very formally. She takes his arm, pretends she's getting out of the limousine in a long

gown and furs. They both walk, standing tall and smiling as though they have an audience.)

Husband: This is a great opening night—look at the crowd!

Wife: Yes, isn't it exciting. Everyone is looking at us— you look so handsome!

Husband: And you look very beautiful. *(He looks at her).* In fact, I've never seen you prettier than you are right now.

Wife: I love it when you say things like that to me with your eyes sparkling like that . . .

Husband *(dialogue is getting real):* Maybe I don't say it often enough . . .

Wife: That never occured to me. You're always so good to me, and reliable. I can always count on you.

Husband *(looking rueful):* I sound like Renfro of the Mounties. Does that make it hard for you to ask anything more of me?

Wife *(looks chagrined):* I guess it does—you do so much . . .

Husband: I was beginning to get a kick out of that charade, maybe I want more, too. What's so terrible about that?

Wife *(hugs him):* I really love you . . .

Husband: Maybe we're ready for something new—let's go on.

Wife: What's your phantasy?

Husband *(closes eyes):* I see a farm with rolling green hills as far as you can see. I'm on a horse, look like a rugged cowboy. I can't see you anywhere . . .

Wife: Does that mean you want to be alone?

Husband: I don't know—I feel kind of peaceful when I look at that scene—a kind of calmness. . . . *(Still has eyes closed, a slight smile on his face.)*

Wife *(watches him for a moment):* You know, I have

mixed feelings. Part of me is jealous and feels left out, but another part of me is saying maybe you need that kind of space right now. Maybe you're at a place in your growth where that's important for you for some reason we won't understand until you try it.

Husband: I don't know—I'll have to think about it.

Wife: It really would be OK with me if you took a weekend or a few days to yourself—go fishing or something—and see how you feel. *(Laughs.)* I might even get more romance if you got what you need right now.

The bond of trust makes it possible for people to explore on this level without being so threatened that they have to close it off. Without the basis of trust, distance feels more like loss than space. When people are able to make deep and intimate contact with each other, the times when they are in different places in their insides make them acutely aware of their separateness and aloneness, by contrast. It is vital that they be able to recognize these times of separateness as necessary to the flow of the relationship, therefore, painful perhaps, but not at all destructive. It is part of the flow in nature that there is always a dark side of the moon. Growth is exciting but also frightening. Pain is unpleasant, but often gives impetus to growth. We all say we want love, but intense feeling often makes us uneasy, especially if we just let ourselves feel it without putting it into immediate action. Therefore, times of separateness and aloneness are necessary if we want to experience the deepest possible intimacy. One is the opposite side of the other—they flow back and forth according to our need at the moment.

Chapter Fourteen:

Supra-Intuitive Communication

The exploration phase as it develops, leads the relationship into what I have found, at least so far, to be the deepest area of connection. This is the area I call, for want of a better term, "supra-intuitive communication." Supra-intuitive communication, in the sense I am using the term, is the ability to communicate without words or body. The irony is that we have to go through all the phases of growth I have discussed in order to get back to the process with which we began our lives. I believe, however, that it is impossible to sustain communication on this level without the structure, trust, and exploration levels I have just described.

Let me explain my supra-intuitive communication by example:

(Couple is at a party, across the room from each other, not facing, talking to others.)

Wife *(turns and walks over to husband)*: Hello, are you all right?

Husband: Why do you ask?

Wife: I was talking to Jack and suddenly I had an image of a small child crying. He looked like you.

Husband *(laughs)*: Well, I don't feel like crying, but I don't feel well. Must be something I had at dinner. I was just debating about whether to suggest we go home.

Wife: Let's go—maybe you're more ill than you think if I picked it up that strongly.

Or:

(Husband and wife are sitting in bed side by side and reading.)

Husband: You know, for a little while I stopped reading and just sat here to see if I could conjure up a picture of what might be going on inside of you. I experienced a kind of light, airy balloon with red and white stripes—does that fit in any way?

Wife: Let me see. *(closes eyes)* Yes, you're right. I feel like a kid who's been to the circus—it was such a lovely day today, full of nice surprises. I can see the red and white balloon, too. Let me see what I can pick up about you. *(Keeps eyes closed, sits awhile without talking.)* I see a small boy and he seems to be sitting on a pier or a hill or something. I can only see his back. His shoulders are slumped and his head is down. The back of his neck looks so vulnerable . . .

Husband *(has tears in his eyes)*: I don't know why I'm crying. I'm not aware that that fits anything I'm thinking or feeling. Let me just stay with it a minute . . .

(Both sit quietly without saying anything.)

Husband: A picture of our son just flashed in my head. I was thinking how proud I am of him and how afraid I am for him. I wish I could protect him from ever getting hurt.

Wife: I guess you carry him around with you inside more than you thought.
Husband: I guess I do—there's something about him that reminds me of you.
Wife: What is that?
Husband: That "red balloon" quality. He and you have a kind of spirit that nothing seems to dampen—life is always exciting and somehow new to you—it's a quality I don't have. I keep plodding, but I get discouraged easily. I sometimes am awed by that quality in you. If I were to lose you, it would be like a light going out for me.

Perhaps, via these examples, you can begin to perceive and to appreciate the depth and the power of this kind of contact. It produces a magic in the connection that is one of the most beautiful experiences in life. As this supra-intuitive communication develops, it becomes possible at times to feel your "insides" touching even though you are not in physical or verbal contact. You become able to explore each other on a level where any kind of defense, game, or subterfuge is not only totally unnecessary, but is ludicrous. When you're talking in words and not getting anywhere, you can drop the words, tune in to your insides and begin to get a picture of what's getting in the way on the basis of this level of communication. When you're feeling sad or in pain or upset, you can feel your partner in touch with you, feeling your feelings with you, but not intruding in any way—just "there" in the inside, where it really counts. There is often a sense of aloneness, but never of loneliness. You develop a kind of rhythm, a flow on this level that, in moments of most intimate contact, feels almost like some kind of mutual dance. It is an awesome experience, the experience that romanticists from the beginning of time have described as magical love, but the nature of which they have not defined. Many people have glimpses of this kind of experience, but are unable to recapture or sustain it because they haven't developed the necessary base. On some level, we are all aware of this kind of potential in us even though we may never have seen or experienced it. We strive for it without knowing what it is we are looking for.

When people get to this depth in a relationship, the process of connecting on this level unleashes tremendous individual creativity. It seems something of a paradox that the deepest possible connection often catapults people into very separate places; however, it is understandable, because such a connection puts each of us in touch with parts of ourselves we never knew existed before.

I am convinced that we have infinite avenues for discovery within ourselves if we but knew all the processes for opening these avenues. I have only described a few. If people begin to develop a relationship on these levels, it is impossible to get bored or restless or disinterested. The possibilities for change, for discovery, for richness are endless on the deepest level. It is as though new life is constantly appearing. A couple will develop the basic structure, then the bond of trust, then the exploration and then the supra-intuitive communication. Then the burst of creativity occurs which catapults each individual into a different place in terms of his knowledge about himself—his depth, his perceptiveness, and his level of awareness. This makes it necessary for them to modify their basic structure to fit the changes in themselves, deepen their bond with new knowledge, expand their exploration to new depths, and extend their communication into more subtle nuances and shades of awareness, and, again, new creativity. It is an evolutionary, never-ending process—always exciting, sometimes fearsome, because the direction is unknown, the future unpredictable. It is, however, satisfying beyond anything else in life.